Contents

The Color Section follows page 92.

4

Dedicated to Mummy. Rest happily on your laurels.
Happy 75th year!

Baltimore Album Quilts

Historic Notes and Antique Patterns

A Pattern Companion to Baltimore Beauties and Beyond

Volume One

by Elly Sienkiewicz

C&T PUBLISHING

Front Cover Photo:
"Wreath and Dove II"
Pattern #55, block D-2, from quilt #2
Detail: Baltimore Album Quilt, Accession #76.609.6. Gift of Mr. and Mrs. Foster McCarl, Jr.
(Photo: Abby Aldrich Rockefeller Folk Art Center, Williamsburg, Virginia)

Photography by Abby Aldrich Rockefeller Folk Art Center, Art Institute of Chicago, Garrison Studios, Jadwinds Studio,
Sylvia Pickell, Sharon Risedorph, Elly Sienkiewicz, Sotheby's Photography Studio, and St. Louis Art Museum.

Edited by Sayre Van Young
Berkeley, California

Illustrations by Julie Olsen, Washington, D.C., and Lisa Krieshok, Berkeley, California

Design/Production Coordination by Bobbi Sloan Design
Berkeley, California

Typesetting by Byron Brown/MACAW
Oakland, California

Published by C&T Publishing
P. O. Box 1456
Lafayette, California 94549

ISBN: 0-914881-35-3 Hardcover
ISBN: 0-914881-28-0 Softcover

Library of Congress Card Number: 89-82563

First Edition

Second Printing

Printed in Hong Kong
by Regent Publishing Services Ltd.

Acknowledgments

Thank you to the needleartists, both those whose work already beautifies this series and those whose work is yet to be seen in *Volumes II* and *III*; to Carolie and Tom Hensley, C&T Publishing, for their game and substantial support of this book; and to Todd Hensley, whose managerial style, as amiable as capable, makes working with him a pleasure.

Thank you to my colleagues in preparing this book, Sayre Van Young, Bobbi Sloan, and Lisa Krieshok, in California, and Julie Olsen, Kathy Mannix, and Lesley Arietti in Washington, all women of exceptional talent for whose input I am grateful and whose professional companionship I've enjoyed.

Thank you to Barbara R. Luck, Curator, and Catherine H. Grosfils, Audiovisual Editorial Librarian, of Colonial Williamsburg's Abby Aldrich Rockefeller Folk Art Center; to Christa Thurman, Textile Curator, and Mickey Wright, Research Assistant, of the Art Institute of Chicago; to Zoe Perkins, Textile Curator, and Patricia Woods, Photography Manager, of the St. Louis Art Museum; and to Barbara Klein, head of Sotheby's Photo Archives, for helping implement the concept of this book.

Thank you to Rev. Edwin Schell, Executive Secretary of the Methodist Historical Society for photographic permission and research aid. Thank you for research aid to Dr. S. Brent Morris, Book Review Editor, *The Scottish Rite Journal*; Stephen Patrick, Curator, George Washington Masonic National Memorial Association; and to Barbara Franco, Curator, Museum of Our National Heritage.

And thank you to Walter Filling once again, for his gracious contribution of the classically calligraphed title page; to the Lunch Bunch (Kathryn Blomgren Campbell, Lois Russell Charles, Christina Sprague, and Ellen Blendheim Stewart) for friendship and festivity; and to my friend and neighbor, Mary Sue Hannan, for a burden lifted. A special thank you to Diane Pedersen, not only for serving so capably as C&T's Marketing Director, but for imparting such good cheer as well.

And thank you, dear family, Donald, Alex, Katya, and Stan.

Introduction

Welcome to *Baltimore Album Quilts—Historic Notes and Antique Patterns*, a pattern companion to *Baltimore Beauties and Beyond, Studies in Classic Album Quilt Appliqué, Volume I.* In the first volume, we began a journey together to bygone Baltimore to study the classic mid-nineteenth-century Baltimore Album Quilts and to learn the methods of their making. To the dozens of appliqué techniques given in that volume, I'll add just one more appliqué approach here, an easy way to succeed with the most complex blocks (see Appendix I). Whether you are a proficient appliquér or just beginning, you should be able to find a pattern perfect for you here.

Rather than simply a how-to text, this book is an intimate visit with the classic Baltimore Album Quilt blocks themselves, and with some of the "beyond" Baltimore quilts as well. Some of the blocks were first seen in quilts in *Volume I.* To those we have added a few more original designs based on classic blocks and a multitude of classic patterns.

One of the most exciting stops on this visit to old Baltimore City will be with what is surely one of the most exquisite antique Baltimore Album Quilts ever made, the sixteen-block quilt from the collection of the Abby Aldrich Rockefeller Folk Art Center (see quilt #2 in the Color Section). In addition, we are introduced to the historically fascinating Album now in the Maryland Historical Society (quilt #3 in the Color Section), and to the beautiful St. Louis Museum of Art's Album (quilt #4 in the Color Section). Our fourth antique quilt, the Art Institute of Chicago's "circa 1845-1850" Album (quilt #1 in the Color Section) is bright and charming, an example of a Maryland-style Album Quilt in which the blocks all have a delightfully naive quality as though made by one or two uniquely individualistic hands.

My own preference is avidly to collect blocks in all the styles of Old Baltimore and to mix them exuberantly in a given Album. But I hope to present diverse block patterns so that you have ample choices for designing your modern masterpiece by whatever approach you prefer. In this book, I've particularly tried to present some of the types of patterns that help visually organize the internal arrangement of blocks within a quilt, an issue discussed in detail in *Volume II.*

Some of you will just be beginning your Album Quilt journey. Others may be well on your way and anxious for the challenge of the fanciest of Album Quilt blocks. Therefore many patterns for the ornate, more realistic Victorian Album designs are presented here along with less complex blocks. Because response to the cutwork appliqué methods which dominated *Volume I* has been so positive, many simpler patterns have been adapted for this method. Most of these color plates show the classic blocks themselves. Their patterns herein are hand drawn from tiny photos. Thus looking closely at the color plates, perhaps even with a magnifier, should reward you with an even better view of the embellishment details. Being hand drawn, these patterns are interpretations and will differ slightly from the blocks themselves. For example, if it seems placement of an appliqué has gotten off-register in the sewing, I've sometimes tried to depict a hypothetically "original pattern" placement. Other times, the actual block is so charming I've just presented it as it is! Move such elements around as you choose. For these patterns, then as now, form a sourcebook for further original design. Motifs from these classic patterns can be used and reused in seemingly endless combinations.

These patterns are drawn to fit a 12½" block. Originally, I chose this size—estimated from a photo—because it was the smallest classic Baltimore Album Quilt block size I'd seen after quilting. Baltimore Album Quilt blocks were sometimes a bit bigger, with 16" to 16½" being a rough average. Perhaps it's just as well I began with the smaller size—its fineness of scale allows a useful freedom with sets and borders. Because most of these patterns almost fill that space (the 12½" size) completely, if you prefer a slightly larger block or would like to leave more background fabric showing, use the patterns as given but cut the finished block a size larger. Or you can enlarge the patterns.

The three Appendices contain a variety of helpful information. The first suggests an easy and foolproof approach to complex pattern appliqué. The second has course descriptions and supply lists for ten classes using this book as a text. Some of these courses are clearly geared towards professional teaching in shops or other forums. Most of them, however, would also serve as an entertaining challenge to Baltimore Album Quilt study groups, or to those of you who are enjoying this excursion to classic Baltimore on your own. And the third appendix lists several sources for books and quilting supplies.

Like *Volume I* itself, this book concentrates on blocks alone. Included in the patterns, though, is one for the medallion four-block center of quilt #7 and quilt #8 from *Volume I*. Analysis of sets and borders, plus a gold mine of border patterns, have been left for *Volume II*. For inspiration, the color pages in this book conclude with two contemporary Album Quilts, one by Ruby Ollivier and another by Esther Rose Jackson (see quilts #5 and #6 in the Color Section). Together with the classic antique quilts, all should conspire (and inspire you) to set your own sights high as you explore the delights of Baltimore and beyond!

How to Use This Book

Baltimore Album Quilts—Historic Notes and Antique Patterns presents fifty-six patterns for making fifty-eight striking blocks. Pattern Notes refer to those techniques in *Volume I* particularly suited to making a given pattern and also offer pertinent background information on each block.

A full-color photo of each pattern's block appears in the Color Section to help you select appliqué fabric. "Part One: Getting Started" in *Volume I* provides important information on how to transfer the patterns (given here on one page, two pages, and four pages) from the book to make your own complete 12½"-square pattern. Four patterns (#32, 33, 34, and 35) are presented on one diagonal half of four pages. To transfer these, simply follow the Third Method,

then the Second Method for pattern transfer, shown in *Volume I*.

The Gallery Quilts, also in the Color Section, exhibit six quilts: four antique and two contemporary. Throughout this book, when a quilt is referred to by number (as quilt #1, or quilt #5), you will find it pictured in the Color Section. And, if you are wondering about the antique quilts and their makers or about the needleartists who worked on the contemporary blocks and quilts pictured, see "Part One: The Quiltmakers."

When a specific block is referred to, for example, as "quilt #4, block D-2," the block can be located by its letter and number: the letters refer to the block position in the quilt, reading from left to right, and the numbers refer to position from top to bottom.

Part One: The Quiltmakers

About the Needleartists Whose Work Appears in *Baltimore Album Quilts—Historic Notes and Antique Patterns.*

While the quiltmakers' names for the four antique Gallery Quilts shown in the Color Section may be uncertain, we can, nevertheless, become more familiar with these women by looking a bit more closely at each quilt.

THE QUILTS
About the Antique Quilts That Appear in the Color Section.

Specific, yet diverse, intentions seem to have inspired the making of the classic Baltimore Album Quilts. So familiar are we with the bride's quilt concept, that for some time, the Baltimore Album Quilts were referred to as "Baltimore Brides' Quilts." While that has proved too narrow a characterization, quilt #1 may indeed be a Bride's Quilt. My sense about quilts #2 and #3 is that they were intended "to remember"—to record or memorialize—significant people and events. Quilt #4 on the other hand, seems to be a charming combination of remembering, or recording, a moment in history and of being an open offering, as well, of friendship's yearning "to be remembered." Adding to its mystery, no written clue inscribed on quilt #2 witnesses either its origin or its intent. Quilt #4, though, like so many Album Quilts, enjoins its recipient, and even those who were to come after, with a calligraphed message to "Forget me not." Numerous other intriguing intents are considered in the notes accompanying the patterns in "Part Two: The Patterns."

QUILT #1: *Baltimore-style Album Quilt*, circa 1845–50. Accession #1957.524. 89¾" x 90⅜". Gift of Mrs. Chauncey B. Borland to the collection of the Art Institute of Chicago, Chicago, Illinois.

Delightfully individualistic, bold in design and brilliant in color, this Album seems tied closely to well-documented Baltimore by recognizable design motifs and such needlework characteristics as its padded appliqué and the "wool and cotton" embroidery. It has extensive wool straight-stitch embroidery over some appliqué edges, and what might be called a whipped satin stitch tightly and decoratively binding others. Some of this is seen in quilt #3 as well and both have versions of a relatively rare block type, a half-circle spray of flowers. Quilt #1 surely captures the drama prize, however, with its rising rampant eagle skywriting this burst of blooms. The basket in block A-4 has a lookalike in quilt #3's block D-5, though its flowers look more like that quilt's block B-5. It shares virtually the same lumpy cornucopia shape (block E-3) with *Volume I*'s Classic Baltimore Album, quilt #4 (block D-1); and block C-1 in both quilts are similar albeit unique. Both blocks share the same yellow calico, are primitive in design, and seem intentionally, if obscurely, symbolic. Both quilts have

what look like variations of an oak leaf and reel block, not very common in Baltimore quilts, although acorns and oak leaves certainly are. And these two quilts may each have Odd Fellow symbolism: the arrows in quilt #1, the moons (?) and stars and the dove in *Volume I*'s quilt #4, and the cornucopias in both.

While one must use caution in speaking definitively about this classic genre, the full extent of which is still unknown, conjecture is certainly enjoyable and potentially rewarding. What sort of Album do you think quilt #1 is? What intents did its maker(s) have? Why put so much creative passion into a quilt? As you read through its pattern notes, perhaps you'll sense, as I did, that romance was surely in the air!

QUILT #2: *Classic Baltimore-style Album Quilt*, circa 1850. Accession #76.609.6. 92" x 91½". Gift of Mr. and Mrs. Foster McCarl, Jr., to the Abby Aldrich Rockefeller Folk Art Center, Williamsburg, Virginia.

Complexly beautiful, this Album seems to have quilted-in secrets yet to be unseen. At first glance strikingly unified in style, it yet hints of a group rather than an individual creation. The top and right borders, for example, are more tightly wound than the other two borders and close inspection shows differing needlework styles from place to place. The beehive which knots the border seems to hold great import as do the four buildings which form one of the most unique and magnificent of Album Quilt medallion centers. Two of these edifices tie the quilt to the classic Album makers' beloved Baltimore City, and a third to their nation and times. The remaining red brick structure faces us with the All-Seeing Eye of God,[1] cleverly symbolized by a fabric print, cutout. This building hints of the mysteries of secret orders,[2] echoed elsewhere in this and other Albums of Old Baltimore.

The border's carefully wrought beehive aswarm with busy bees is not a simple issue either, for, symbol of the subordinate Odd Fellow lodge, The Obligated Daughters of Rebekah,[3] it is also an ancient symbol of the Free and Accepted Masons. The symbol of the All-Seeing Eye of God, too, was held in common by Odd Fellows and Masons. To speak of which order is here intended requires much further investigation. Freemasons, however, were a critical ceremonial link in the monumental architecture of this country from its inception through the early decades of the nineteenth century. The ceremony of September 18, 1793,[4] when George Washington declared the cornerstone of the nation's Capitol "well and truly laid," was an exciting one, oft repeated in those decades of rapid growth in Baltimore City as well as in Washington. Music sounded, artillery salutes reverberated, Masons in full regalia stood by, and the City's most prominent Mason, like George Washington, would have been there with a sterling silver trowel to "spread the cement of brotherly love." The laying of cornerstones blessed by Masonic ritual nurtured the vision of a new enlightened order held by Americans, Mason and non-Mason alike, and bespoke propitious beginnings. Not until a scandal precipitated the anti-Masonic movement of the 1830s, fueling fears of the secret societies, were Masons less a visible part of national life. That this quilt dated later (rightly I believe), "circa 1850," yet hints so strongly of secret orders, should be taken seriously.

Of recorded history, though, this quilt speaks eloquently enough. Block C-3 may in fact be the Capitol[5] in Washington, our nation's "ennobling shrine." The view here seems to be the West Front, high on Jenkins Hill. Patriotism and beauty would be reason enough for its inclusion, but its presence might also be intended to symbolize the role of Baltimore (and possibly that of Freemasonry?) in the young nation's history. Then, too, the beloved Capitol, already once so devastated in the War of 1812, was about to undergo a major change. A new dome would be erected, and a contest for its design was to be held in 1850. Perhaps the Album blockmaker wanted to honor the Capitol as she had known it all her life, and to memorialize architect Charles Bullfinch who had died in 1844 and whose dome had given the Capitol this look from 1825–56. Our appliqué portraitist may also have wished to memorialize George Washington, Father of Our Country, who laid the cornerstone, and Charles Carroll of Carrollton, first Senator from Maryland, last surviving signer of the Declaration of Independence, and Baltimore's most illustrious citizen (and most prominent Mason) who had died in 1832. Surely this quilt proudly records important times, recently lived through.

Grandly displaying monumental architecture as it does, this quilt itself seems a monument to momentous history. Today history is recorded in snapshots and on videotapes, but photography would have been the youngest of fledglings at the time of this quilt's making. The older of the ladies making quilts in Baltimore, quiltmakers such as Achsah Goodwin Wilkins (1775–1854),[6] would have lived through the Revolutionary War, the War of 1812, the Mexican War, and then the threat of war over how territories should enter the Union, slave or free. Such women had lived through portentous times. They knew, verily, that the city and the citizens of Baltimore had played a role on history's cusp and had played it courageously, victoriously. Survival of America, this "great experiment," had been repeatedly threatened, and, as this quilt reminds us, Baltimore was America's great heroine. One Baltimore quiltmaker had dated her quilt on the back "1852" (perhaps to remember its completion) then had in careful red cross-stitch inscribed "Baltimore" and "1776" (the Declaration of Independence) and "1784" (ratification of the Treaty of Paris, ending the Revolutionary War). This at the center of her glorious, seemingly once-in-a-lifetime quilt. (See quilt #1 in *Volume I*.)

This unknown quiltmaker seems to have intended to stitch an heirloom Album to reflect Baltimore's heroic role in her nation's history, an Album by which "to remember." Both the older women and women as young as Mary Evans's (1829–1916)[7] generation would, at this quilt's making, most likely have sent loved ones off to fight yet again for the Union and for the new state of Texas against the Mexican government. Or, if 1848 or after, they would have been rejoicing at another war over, another victory won, and mourning their fallen. With the thought that this quilt itself might be a monument, a memorial, let's look at the history which, though uninscribed upon this quilt, seems nonetheless so clearly represented within its borders.

Consider, first, the history represented by our Capitol. The British sacking of the Capitol in the War of 1812 was an act of pure vandalism of which even they were later openly ashamed. The burning of the White House, some private residences, and the wanton despoiling of the Congressional library and public records in the Capitol inflamed patriots who claimed "that Cockburn himself had led a detachment of troops into the House Chamber. They said he took over the Speaker's chair and put the rhetorical question, 'Shall this harbor of Yankee democracy be burned?' The motion carried with a roar of 'ayes' and piles of ignitables in both the Senate and House wings were torched."[8] After August 25, 1814, abandoning ravaged Washington City, the British force sailed up the Patuxent to attack prosperous Baltimore in the Battles of North Point and Fort McHenry. Expecting just that, Baltimore had its militia mustered. Victorious in those two battles, Baltimore was critical in turning the war around.[9] Justly proud, Baltimoreans memorialized the valor and the victory in two monuments. One, known as the Battle Monument, stands proudly in this quilt (block C-2), still protectively close to the Capitol.

Our Capitol and the Baltimore Monument to George Washington (block B-3) occur repeatedly in these classic quilts, but never more elegantly depicted than here. Let's visit with Old Baltimore City, then, guided by these two beautifully wrought building portraits and listen to what they tell us of Baltimore's story.

The block portraying the Baltimore Monument to George Washington reflects this history. In 1809, the tenth anniversary of George Washington's death, some prominent Baltimore citizens applied to the Maryland legislature for a lottery to raise $100,000 to erect a monument to memorialize the first president. Six years and the intervention of the War of 1812 later, a crowd estimated at between 20,000 and 30,000 assembled at the monument's site, Howard's Woods, to watch the Most Worshipful Master and lesser dignitaries of the Masonic order lay the cornerstone for the edifice. "Divine Providence," wrote one chronicler, "seemed to smile upon the occasion, the air was delightfully cool, and the firmament serene."[10] Such were the beginnings of the first monument in the United States to do honor to the Father of Our Country. That the Album Quilt makers were inordinately proud of this monument is witnessed by its frequent portrayal in these quilts.

The most critical moment in Baltimore's history is also remembered in this quilt. It had occurred on September 12 and 13, 1814, when the city was attacked first by land, then by sea. In the aftermath, the Committee of Vigilence and Safety determined to build a memorial to perpetuate the memory of those who had given their lives fighting for the city. When ground was broken for this second, though simpler, monument to George Washington within months of the first, Baltimore earned the name, "The Monumental City." During this same period, two other monuments, the Battle Monument and the Armistead Monument, were erected. The first honors those slain in the land Battle of North Point; the second honors Lieutenant Colonel George Armistead, in command of Fort McHenry on that dreadful night immortalized in "The Star-Spangled Banner."[11] The ceremonial laying of the cornerstones for each of these monuments was presided over by Masons, as was the custom of the time, and accompanied by great public celebrations.

In major American and European cities, this was the "Cities Beautiful" period when much of the monumental architecture we admire today was built. The fifty-two-foot-high Battle Monument, designed by Maximillian Godefroy, the city's leading architect, consists of a column rising above a pedestal upon an Egyptian pyramidal base. Four eagles perch on the corners of the first tier and a ten-foot statue of a lady, representing the City of Baltimore, rises above all. Clearly she was more than the Album block's maker, however skilled, wanted to deal with. The monument was adopted in 1827 as the city's seal and forms the center of its flag, imposed upon Lord Baltimore's black and gold colors.

Furthermore, after the death of Andrew Jackson in 1845, inclusion of the Battle Monument in an Album Quilt such as quilt #2 might possibly be intended to memorialize "Old Hickory" as well. He had gained national adulation as the hero of the Battle of New Orleans in 1815, the battle that signaled the final British defeat and ended the War of 1812. In *Old Quilts* (Plate 48), Dr. Dunton records a Baltimore-style Album with a direct and clear Jacksonian reference. The block, the center one, is similar to "Cherry Wreath with Bluebirds" (Pattern #31). "In upper left: Andrew Jackson. In upper right: Victory at N.O. Jan. 8th, 1815. In centre: 'The Blessing of Government, like the dew

of Heaven, should be equally dispersed on the rich and poor.' A.J.W. Jacson [*sic*]." Perhaps significantly, that quilt duplicates four blocks and needlework styles from quilt #3 which also has a center block memorializing a fallen war hero.[12]

Two rather elegant Victorian gas lights flank this Battle Monument, proudly symbolizing Baltimore's progress and prosperity. As the nation's second largest seaport in a mercantile era, Baltimore had all the latest amenities, including as early as 1820, the newly discovered illuminating gas.[13] Surely such proud affirmations of the "Age of Progress" seem to imply that Baltimore's quiltmakers believed that "Future ages will wonder at us, as the present age wonders at us now."[14] And is it not so? Much in these quilts looks backward at the fullness of momentous history gently receding and memorializes its departing heros. But there is a savoring in these quilts as well, of the excitement of modernization, of industrialization, of the power of progress and urban prosperity, of the dearness of friendship and fellowship. For surely these quiltmaking women watched uneasily the storm clouds scudding above. The approaching Civil War promised fearful times ahead for the nation they so fervently loved and for which they had fought so hard, working together for their community like the symbolic bees on the quilt's border. Keeping most of her mysteries still, quilt #2 is one of Old Baltimore's most fascinating ladies. Her reticence to speak plainly, undeniably part of her Victorian charm, is no doubt made the more maddening for her being, still, so opulently beautiful.

QUILT #3: *Classic Baltimore Album Quilt* inscribed, in part, "Mrs. John Mann, Eutaw Street, Baltie," circa 1845–50. Sold at Sotheby's "Important Americana" Auction in January 1988, and now in the collection of the Maryland Historical Society in Baltimore, Maryland.

This quilt descended in the family of Mrs. Henry Richmond until the Twardowicz family of Baltimore won it by chance at a Carmelite auction earlier in this century. Its early provenance comes to us through Dunton's *Old Quilts* where he seems to pass on family tradition that at an "album quilt party" in 1845, friends of Mrs. Henry Richmond brought along the blocks on which they had expended their skill and their affection for Mrs. Richmond. Expressing the custom felicitously, Dunton explains in *Old Quilts* (pp. 17–19), "The practice of giving individual blocks for quilts with the idea of having the whole recall friends to the owner had its counterpart in the autograph album."

Quilt #3 ranks as an important classic Baltimore Album Quilt. Like quilt #1, it is characterized by a quantity of wool embroidery. This is "relatively rare" in an Album Quilt, in Dr. Dunton's opinion, and reflects the "German influence." One particularly elegant wool and silk embroidered block, with a

Dresden-style vase and padded roses similar to those in block C-2, was saved from the quilt and framed, according to Mrs. Richmond's family. Block E-2 in quilt #10 (*Volume II*) is so similar, and the block's appearance so rare, that judged by photos at least, they must surely be related. And the woolwork? German-origin Berlin work, a needlework rage in both England and America by the 1840s, must have influenced some Baltimore quiltmakers. Their favorite fancywork was clearly quilts, but quilts so impressively abreast of, and reflective of, their times that they sometimes read like a history book. In Berlin work, Merino or zephyr wool was worked primarily on canvas and was a bit like today's needlepoint with an extensive stitch vocabulary and a wealth of printed designs.[15] So too, seemingly the most common wool stitch in the Album Quilt is a straight stitch: worked perpendicular to the appliqué seam (or slanted at an angle along it) or worked in a patterned combination of long and short stitches.

German immigrants or descendants, both fueling and inspired by Baltimore's appliquéd Album phenomenon, may indeed have influenced the incorporation of wool embroidery into the appliqué. Confirming German heritage certainly, Dunton notes that Henry Richmond had been born "Reichman" in Strasburg, Germany, and that Mrs. Richmond's maiden name was Mary Seesnop. He records that the couple married in the German Reformed Church in Baltimore and later joined the Emory Methodist Church (*Old Quilts*, p. 20). Dena Katzenberg suggests that Mrs. Richmond, Mrs. Mann (whose name is inscribed on block C-2), and Mary Evans (connected to these quilts in the Dunton *Notebooks*) all attended religious classes together, and were Methodists of the East Baltimore Station (*Baltimore Album Quilts*, p. 84).

One senses a strong design hand in this quilt. From the pre-planned, boldly elegant rose and bud border with its perfectly turned corners, to the beautiful balance of similarly functioning, yet differing block designs in virtually all directions, it has the aura of a quilt which may have received major group contributions but where perhaps only one person had the last word in what went in and where it went. The set of this quilt seems particularly carefully and successfully designed with an eye to focusing on block C-2 and then on C-3, the true center block.

Four strong diagonal blocks anchor the outermost corners of the quilt and the touches of pink, royal blue, and yellow, which accent the dominant red and green color scheme, fall almost without exception in the central three block by five block vertical panel. The central monument block, the most ornately embellished of the quilt, is in a place of honor. Here with a fruited tree overhead, and in other versions labeled "Ringgold,"[16] this appears to be an outdoor monument or tomb. Major Samuel Ringgold was born to an early Baltimore family prominent in both the Masons and in the military. Beloved by Baltimore's citizenry, he was killed May 8, 1846, helping to defeat a group of Mexicans at the Battle of Palo Alto.[17] Barely four months later, at the Battle of Monterrey, another of Baltimore's sons, Lieutenant Colonel William H. Watson caught a bullet in the neck and was killed instantly. Dubbed the "gallant Watson," he had already served Baltimore well as a lawyer, city councilman, and Speaker of the House of Delegates and now had sacrificed his own life to serve Texas and the nation.

The central memorial block (C-2) might read as an eulogy, with the cherry tree conveying Sweet Character and Good Deeds, and the rose for Love (a single rose for Simplicity and, if Masonic, for Temperance). The eulogy echoes the words of Pericles's Funeral Oration, "Where the rewards of valor are the greatest, there you will find also the best and bravest spirits among the people." Recalling those very sentiments, an exquisite block, block E-2, is inscribed: "To the Gray Boys/Guardians of Freedom, of Justice and Virtue; Citizens, Soldiers of Liberty's Soil/This token of friendship I gladly present you,/Then guard it from insult and shield it from spoil/Strong be the links in the chain of our union/And never the Soldier's proud precept forsake;/Long may you live in a martial communion;/And scorn'd be the slavery who the compact would break./M.A.B."

Underlying the whole issue of the Mexican War, in Maryland as well as throughout the country, was the compelling question of how territories would enter the Union, as slave states or free. Is that the question the quiltmaker is addressing in the wreathed inscription? Or does her reference express her fervent wish that her fellow Americans settled in Texas be free from thralldom to Mexico and one with the Union?

Tying that which this quilt remembers even closer to the Mexican War, Dr. Dunton relates that not only was that extra Dresden-style vase block set aside from this quilt, but there was as well a second quilt of the same vintage in Mrs. Richmond's family. Its focus is a monument block with the name "Watson" and his death date, 1846, appliquéd above it.

It seems as though these quilts might each have been made to memorialize one of the two Baltimore heroes killed just four months apart in the Mexican War. What motivated such passion in Baltimore over the War? Why would quiltmakers have stitched its losses, and eventually its gains (Texas) into their quilts? To understand a bit better, one has to savor that history for a moment, and to contemplate the notions of "honor" and "glory" through their eyes.

The Republic of Texas was admitted to the Union as the twenty-eighth state on July 4, 1845. Historian James McSherry notes dryly that this was "an act, which, in view of the fact that Mexico had never relinquished her claim to the territory, was tantamount to a declaration of war. Neither country shrank from the encounter."[18] The shot that started the hostilities must have roused anger in Baltimore, for it killed a Marylander, Colonel Trueman Cross, quartermaster general in the army, who was attacked by "banditi" while he was innocently (war not yet having been declared) "riding out for exercise." In a special message to Congress on May 11, President Polk announced that "American blood had been shed upon American soil, and that by the acts of her generals, Mexico had proclaimed that hostilities had commenced." By May 13, Congress had declared war. In short order, Maryland's governor responded to Polk's call for volunteers by summoning the state's citizens between 18 and 45 years of age to enlist.

The campaign in the Southwest proved exceptionally popular and the two regiments called for from Baltimore filled rapidly. One winces today at Walt Whitman's harshness when he wrote that it was time for the world to see that "America knows how to crush, as well as how to expand." Nonetheless, the women who wove symbols of the "highest levels of benevolence," friendship, love, patriotism, and religious devotion into the classic Baltimore Album Quilts also peppered them with what reads as real enthusiasm for the Mexican War. This, during the same period when Henry David Thoreau in Massachusetts was spending time in jail rather than pay his poll tax which supported the war (an experience he would write up in *Civil Disobedience*), and abolitionist William Lloyd Garrison actually publicly "wished for America's defeat." Still another area of opposition to the war came from anti-slavery congressmen such as Ohio's Joshua Giddings, worried that adding Texas would extend the area of slavery.

"The Battalion of Baltimore and Washington Volunteers" embarked from Washington for Brazos Santiago on June 13, 1845. It was comprised of four companies recruited from Baltimore and two from Washington, few men in total from all the Baltimore volunteers. By September 1, General Zachary Taylor was prepared to march against Monterrey. He led an army "which both in numbers and in spirit proved sufficient for the achievement of victories which added glory to the American arms and thrilled the United States with enthusiasm."[19] Against a strong Mexican position and under deadly volleys, the men marched into the city. At the end of the day, General Garland led his men, which included the Baltimore battalion, away from the fray. Colonel Watson returned to fight again after a full day under fire, and fell dead at the end of just one day of doing battle at Monterrey. His death followed close upon that of Baltimore's Major Ringgold who had also courageously heeded the call for help from "that erstwhile little republic, whose name had become illustrious through the fame of the deeds of Houston and that band of hardy pioneers to whose Americanism the acquisition of Texas is to be credited."[20]

Monterrey stood for four days, then fell. On September 25, tribute was paid to the Baltimore contingent's valor. The "patriotic women of Baltimore," among whom must have numbered some Album quiltmakers, had presented the embarking battalion with an American flag (almost certainly handsewn). On that day it was raised to wave triumphantly where Mexican colors had minutes before flown, from the tower of the Bishop's palace. "It was not an empty honor which was accorded to the men of Maryland for not only had their valor been illustrious but their losses had been severe." Major Buchanan, a hero of the War of 1812 Battle of North Point, replaced Watson, declaring that "A native of Baltimore and a citizen of Washington, his only desire was to make the battalion worthy of the cities that sent it forth." After May 30, the Baltimore battalion was mustered out of service and returned home "with a record of achievement which won for them the gratitude of the people of their native state. On July 10, under fitting circumstances the flag which had floated from Monterrey was presented to the city of Baltimore and accepted in behalf of its citizens by Mayor Davies."[21]

And what of the real relationship of Mrs. Richmond, Mrs. Mann, and possibly their young fellow parishioner, Mary Evans, to this quilt? Ahh, now that's a secret, too, and one still securely sewn between those layers! Could this quilt still be the Friendship Album presented to Mrs. Richmond at an "Album party"? Yes, possibly. To a quiltmaker, receiving a gift of blocks is, in the deepest sense, a "helping hand." And believing in such gestures of friendship it seems, permeated the very air of bygone Baltimore.

QUILT #4: *Classic Baltimore Album Quilt*, inscribed, in part, "Ladies of Baltimore" and "1848." Accession #1:1973. Gift of Mrs. Stratford Lee Morton. (Photo: St. Louis Art Museum)

A classic Baltimore Album Quilt in the grand style, this quilt speaks exuberantly well for itself. With an elegant flourish, it finishes our Gallery Tour of classic Baltimore Beauties as though with a visit to a delightful, long-familiar friend. For this quilt seems clearly to be a Friendship Album, the Belle of the Album genre. The Friendship Album is easily understandable to our own experience and so, like a favorite cousin, dear to us. But this cousin captures our imagination. Showing off modish block styles from simple to exotic, offering heartfelt remembrances, lavishly wrapping this magnificent mélange in intertwined garlands of roses, swishing it all in an airy set before us, she leaves an almost visceral scent in the air of our memory. Surely she doesn't need us to speak for her, trying to reduce this refined delight into words. Let's simply savor her company. We'll seek to know her the more by listening to the sentiments quietly penned on her blocks and meticulously[22] recorded by the St. Louis Museum of Art, where she now resides. For even with illegible spaces, made so by time or archaic calligraphy, these passages have the charm of something old and cherished and tell us more.

A-1: From one of the Rough and Ready/To the/ Worthy President/Mary Ann Hudgins/1848
B-2: Mary Jane Smith/1848
C-2: Friendship's Offering/This is friendship's Offering, whose silent/Eloquence, are richer than words/ Speak of the givers Faith and _____/in all _____ and says Forget me not.

Feliza Garrett

D-2: Friendship's Gift/ Wilt thou kindly accept/This Tribute from me./ _____ not Forget/It was given to Thee/By one who has friendship for God/whose great desire for thy welfare shall be.

_____Garrett

C-3: Presented to E. Morrison/by Ladies of Baltimore, Md./ /Flag of our Union/[inscription in banderole: _____/ _____]
[Then four double rows of signatures:]

_____	_____
_____	_____
_____	_____
_____	_____ Friends

D-4: Laura _____

Flowery expressions of Friendship and an historic, if brief, Happy Ending close our tour. For the salutation, "From one of the Rough and Ready, To the Worthy President — Mary Ann Hudgins, 1848" resounds with unabashed patriotism and nationalistic pride. Perhaps one of Mary Ann's family was one of the brave Baltimoreans who had served under the victorious general. For whatever reason, there is no doubt that Mary Ann, for one, seems ready to support her men and her nation wherever the "Manifest Destiny" may take them. Profound gratitude and great promise must have been on the minds of many Baltimore women, not Mary's alone. For February 2, 1848, the year she signed her quilt, witnessed the signing of the Treaty of Guadalupe Hidalgo and an end to the three-year-long Mexican War, a war to which Baltimore had contributed so selflessly. Then, too, the election of November 1848, saw General Zachary Taylor (who, in Arthur Schlesinger's view, "had nearly won the war single-handedly") elected on the Whig ticket as President. Stocky of build, brave and durable, he had earned the hero's nickname, "Old Rough and Ready." As surely as if she'd kissed him on the cheek while saying it, Mary Ann's message seems to be, "I'm with you all the way, Mr. President!" In classic Baltimore Album tradition, Mary Ann's block would seem to memorialize an exciting moment in history. For President Taylor died suddenly in 1850, after only one-and-a-half years in office. On the table for his consideration were the measures that would become the Compromise of 1850. Just as he did not survive to decide on these issues, the Compromise itself was not strong enough to save the nation from its downward slide into the Civil War— a war that would kill more Americans than World War I and II and the Vietnam War, combined. But the moment Mary Ann had footnoted was a happy one and one whose remembering in her quilt must surely have pleased Mistress Morrison, who would seem to have been the honored recipient of a magnificent gift of friendship.

THE QUILTMAKERS
About the Contemporary Needleartists Whose Work Appears in *Baltimore Album Quilts—Historic Notes and Antique Patterns*.

A contest was held in 1984 asking entrants to reproduce, or base a block on, a design from the book *Spoken Without a Word*. There were ten winners; their names are listed in *Volume I*. These latter-day "Good Ladies of Baltimore" were soon joined by other needleartists, including master quilters. Their enthusiasm and generosity have been essential to all the volumes of *Baltimore Beauties and Beyond*. Note, however, that these brief biographical notes tend to appear only once for each needleartist, though their needlework appears in several of the volumes. Please make the acquaintance of those modern day Good Ladies of Baltimore whose work appears in this book....

BETTY ALDERMAN, Palmyra, New York: design of Betty Alderman's *Scherenschnitte*.
"I have always been doing something with a needle," writes Betty. From studying art at Syracuse University, to knitting and stitching, to owning a yarn shop, to the dramatically successful sort of design we enjoy in this block, Betty is clearly a needleartist. She designed this block for a magnificent friendship quilt, a gift from employees, customers, students, and friends for Laurene Sinema, owner of The Quilted Apple, the quiltshop in Phoenix where Betty worked for two years.

GEORGIA CIBUL, Wilmette, Illinois: Fleur-de-Lis Medallion II.
Like so many of us, Georgia learned her stitchery with her grandmother, doing embroidery when she was six or seven. She moved from samplers, to crewel, to knitting, and finally to quilting some fifteen years ago. As well as raising two daughters ("who don't quilt because I do that"), she does her husband's bookkeeping, has worked at Cottonpatch Fabrics, and continues to love handwork, including miniatures (dolls and doll houses) as well as quiltmaking of all sorts.

GEORGANNA CLARK, Lenexa, Kansas: Cherry Wreath with Bluebirds II.

A quilter for thirty years, Georganna took up patchwork and appliqué in the past fifteen years. While making this block she had been caring for her mother-in-law, a cancer patient, in their home. "A full-time job," Georganna writes. "I find great comfort in quiltmaking." (Thalia Norma Cain died on October 22, 1989, and her name is now enscribed on Georganna's block.)

SHIRLEY BERTOLINO HEDMAN, Schenectady, New York. Cherry Wreath with Bluebirds II.

Shirley began quilting, "a love that never stops growing," in 1973. Active in two guilds, Shirley teaches quiltmaking through adult education classes and Country Cottons Quiltshop. Writing fondly of her husband and three grown children, she notes making some twenty bed quilts for those she loves; she is now making landscape quilts.

ESTHER ROSE JACKSON, Warwick, Rhode Island. "Esther's Baltimore Album."

Always a sewer, Esther remembers first becoming interested in quilting "decades ago" through *McCall's Magazine* and participation in her church women's sewing circle which "had a regular sewing assignment for the missionaries. We made complete baby layettes, clothes, and quilts." A prize-winning quiltmaker, she describes herself as "primarily a rug-hooker" who loves color. Used to working from black-and-white patterns, she enjoyed imposing her own color sense on the patterns in *Spoken Without a Word*.

LUCY ROGERS MATTEO, Pembroke Lakes, Florida: Cherry Wreath with Bluebirds II.

"The part I always liked best about clothing construction was the handwork. So, when I learned to appliqué, I fell madly in love with the process. I'm sure I inherited the love from my mother." Mother would be proud, for Lucy's appliqué, smooth of seam and fine of stitch, is distinctively exquisite! Lucy is a very active member of the West Broward Quilt Guild, and participates generously in group quilts.

MARY WISE MILLER, Raytown, Missouri: Hearts and Swans II.

In the summer of 1989, Mary won three top awards at the Missouri State Fair for a quilt, "Roses for Shanna," made for her granddaughter. It seems fitting, for she was walking Shanna in a baby carriage at a quilt show just ten years ago when her interest in quilting was just beginning. While most of her quilts are made for family, Mary has contributed her remarkable needleartistry to Hallmark publications as well as to *Baltimore Beauties*.

RUBY OLLIVIER, Bakersfield, California: Ruby's Appliquéd Album, quilt #4 in the Color Section.

"I am a disabled veteran of World War II," writes Ruby. "I love all kinds of needlework and crafts and belong to five quilt clubs that cater to my hobbies. My first love is quilting. I also dabble in quilted clothing design and have won many ribbons and awards. At this time I am studying for my Mastercraftsman Certification in quilting."

GERRI RATHBUN, Independence, Missouri: Fleur-de-Lis Medallion I.

"I am a fifth-generation quilter. My great-grandmother Maxwell quilted. My mother pieced her first quilt at age eight and is still quilting. I have never slept under anything but a quilt (except an electric blanket!) but didn't start quilting until I was past forty." Gerri enjoys piecing and appliquéing better than quilting. Enjoying a talent for motivating others, she teaches and lectures on quilting professionally and has "hundreds of quilts to quilt in my head."

MAXINE DAVIS SATCHELL, Hollywood, Florida: Lyre *Scherenschnitte*.

"My mother taught me to make doll clothes when I was confined to bed with measles before kindergarten. I've been sewing ever since. I especially love embroidery, counted cross-stitch, and appliqué. Actually, anything involving a needle—from needleart to crochet and knitting, dressmaking, braided rugs, dollmaking, and upholstering furniture—is my favorite."

DONNA SCRANTON, Independence, Missouri: Betty Alderman's *Scherenschnitte*.

"I've sewn since my daughter, now twenty-five, was born. From sewing her dresses I went on in the past fourteen years to teaching quiltmaking. I teach three classes a week: Basic Sampler and Advanced Sampler, Pennsylvania Dutch, and White on White. My favorite part is seeing people realize that they can do it. Beyond quiltmaking, I've been active in my church and in working with a senior high school class.

ELLY SIENKIEWICZ, Washington, D. C.: Fleur-de-Lis II, Hearts and Tulips, Red Vases and Red Flowers, Asymmetrical Spray of Red Blossoms I, Fleur-de-Lis with Rosebuds III (and inking of IV), Roses for Hans Christian Andersen, Grapevine Lyre Wreath, Cherry Wreath with Bluebirds I (and inking of II), Victorian Favorite, and inking of Fleur-de-Lis Medallion I and II and of Hearts and Swans II.

Originally a high school history and English teacher, Elly has been professionally involved in quiltmaking for 16 years. She began teaching quiltmaking in her home with three young children, then started the mail-order business Cabin Fever Calicoes (with partner Betty Martin) and ran it for seven years. Now she teaches and writes on quiltmaking.

ALBERTINE VEENSTRA, Acton, Massachusetts: Albertine's Rose Climber (her original design).

Born and raised in Altrier, Grand Duchy Du Luxembourg, Albertine began learning sewing from her paternal grandmother when only four. She continued to learn as a young child from the professional seamstresses in her neighborhood. As a young woman, she trained for five years with the Association of Professions in Luxembourg City to become a couturiere. To obtain the final degrees, she served a four-year apprenticeship in Brussels, Belgium. Having arrived in the United States in 1961, Mrs. Veenstra has been quilting (and designing) regularly since 1976.

NOTES

[1] The All-Seeing Eye of God is a symbol of the Master Mason degree. Jeremy Cross's *The True Masonic Chart* (New Haven, 1824) gives this meaning for the symbol: "All-Seeing Eye, whom the Sun, Moon, and Stars obey, and under whose watchful care even Comets perform their stupendous revolutions, pervades the inmost recesses of the human Heart, and will reward us according to our merits" (p. 39).

Rev. T. G. Beharrell, in the *Odd Fellows Monitor and Guide* (Robert Douglass, Indianapolis, 1878), adds "This emblem presents, as one of its first thoughts, the idea of secrecy. The fellowship into which we come on admission into the Order of Odd Fellows is a secret fellowship.... This impressive emblem tells us that the All-Seeing Eye of God is ever upon us.... There is a circle of rays surrounding the eye intended to teach us, and impress our minds with the grandeur and glory of the being whom it is intended to represent" (pp. 36–38).

[2] This building, framed by tropical-looking foliage and emblazoned with the All-Seeing Eye, may picture Solomon's Temple, central to Masonic symbolism and a popular early nineteenth-century needlework subject. Betty Ring in *American Needlework Treasures* (Dutton, New York, 1987) points out that Solomon's Temple was an overwhelmingly popular design on nineteenth-century English samplers. The version (labeled "Solomon's Temple") that she refers to (p. 52) resembles more closely block E-3 of *Volume I*'s quilt #2 than block B-2 in this quilt. However, since no one knew what Solomon's Temple really looked like, imagination in depicting it could be given free rein. Offering further possibilities for what this building might be, Ms. Ring states, "Public buildings and elegant homes are pictured on an important group of Baltimore samplers worked in the 1820s, and the tradition continued until the close of the schoolgirl-needlework era" (p. 87). We can see in the rendering of Pattern #50 a design conceit of enlarged bird and flower which may tie that Album Quilt block to lingering influences of the schoolgirl sampler tradition in Maryland as well. Note: S. Brent Morris, Executive Secretary emeritus of The Philalethes Society (a group doing Masonic research) notes that two globe-topped columns usually characterize depictions of Solomon's Temple and are absent in this block. But he points out the temple pictured on the frontispiece to Edward T. Schultz's *History of Freemasonry in Maryland, from the Earliest Time to the Present* (volume III, Mediary & Company, Baltimore, 1887). Captioned simply "Masonic Temple in Baltimore," it shows an All-Seeing Eye of God emblazoning that temple's pediment. Although that building's portrait bears little resemblence to block B-2, its very existence seems perhaps significant.

[3] Jeremy Cross, *The True Masonic Chart*: "The Bee Hive is an emblem of industry, and recommends the practice of that virtue.... It teaches us, that as we came into the world rational and intelligent beings, so we should ever be industrious ones; never sitting down contented while our fellow-creatures around us are in want, when it is in our power to relieve them, without inconvenience to ourselves.... It might have pleased the Great Creator of heaven and earth, to have made man independent of all other beings; but, as dependence is one of the strongest bonds of society, mankind were made dependent on each other for protection and security, as they thereby enjoy better opportunities of fulfilling the duties of reciprocal love and friendship. Thus was man formed for social and active life, the noblest part of the work of God; and he that will so demean himself, as not to be endeavoring to add to the common stock of knowledge and understanding, may be deemed a *drone* in the *hive* of nature, a useless member of society, and unworthy of our protection as masons" (pp. 38–39).

Rev. T. G. Beharrell, in the *Odd Fellows Monitor and Guide*, adds "The obligated Daughters of Rebekah see in [the Beehive] a lesson of active, earnest and constant work. The Beehive emblems the Rebekah Degree Lodge. The hive sets forth the Lodge and the bees the busy members of the Lodge.... As life is passing, we are taught by the emblem of the Beehive industriously to do the work of life, and for the purpose of helping each other we are banded together in Lodges. It is so much easier to do much of the work of life with associates than it is to do it alone.... As the bees composing a hive are all workers, so we may learn that there should be no drones in a Lodge. Every member of the degree should be a real worker" (pp. 59–60).

[4] Some sense of the festivities can be garnered from this description by the United States Capitol Historical Society of that day in Washington City:

"The day's program involved elaborate Masonic ceremonies, a common practice then, with roots going back to the link between medieval stonemasons and the order. As President, war hero, and Acting Grand Master of Maryland's Grand Lodge, Washington had the lead role, supported by a uniformed and decorated cast from the Alexandria Volunteer Artillery and Masonic lodges of Maryland, Virginia, and the District. A parade began with the President's arrival on the Virginia shore of the "Grand River Patowmack," crossed to the Maryland side, and moved on to the President's Square, collecting additions at each meeting place."

There, Washington, wearing a Masonic apron reputed to be "the handiwork of Mrs. General Lafayette," conducted the ceremony with a marble-headed gavel and a silver trowel. In laying the cornerstone, he placed it on a silver plate marking the date as the 13th year of American independence, the first year of his second term, and the year of Masonry 5793.

" 'The ceremony ended in prayer, Masonic chanting Honours, and a fifteen gun volley from the Artillery,' the *Alexandria Gazette* informed its readers. 'The whole company retired to an extensive booth, where an ox of 500 pounds' weight was barbequed, of which the company generally partook, with every abundance of other recreation' " (United States Capitol Historical Society, *We the People*, Washington, D.C., 1964, pp. 21–22).

[5] See *Baltimore Beauties and Beyond, Volume I*, p. 106 (Photo 30). This block (C-5 from quilt #2 in the Color Section) shows what appears to be the East Front of the Capitol with Bullfinch's dome, from 1825–56. If so, it is a rendering whose stylization keeps closer to the original building than does block C-3, here in quilt #2. I am less sure about block C-3 here being the Capitol than is Dena Katzenberg (*Baltimore Album Quilts*, Baltimore Museum of Art, 1981, p. 54), but some resemblance is there and the inclusion of the Capitol in this quilt makes sense.

Note: Concerning quilt #2, in *Volume I* (p. 106), I also wrote, "Further research into this quilt's picture blocks may focus its date a bit better. For example, block A-3 appears to be a reference to William Henry Harrison's 1840 "Log cabin and hard cider" presidential campaign, while block E-3 looks like the new dome and wing units chosen by contest in 1850 to enlarge the Capitol." I have since decided that the very intentional "smoke stacks" in E-3 make this last identification questionable. Unless these architectural elements were in the plans but never built, this would seem to have to be some different building. Faced with having so to simplify, it is unlikely that a quiltmaker would add something not there. With its exotic look, perhaps this might be meant to represent Solomon's Temple?

If block C-3 in quilt #2 is the Capitol, it cannot be the East Front, for the pediment over the central portion is such an important, easily rendered detail. The central portion of the West Front is the only visible exterior remnant of Bullfinch's design today. The first photograph of the Capitol shows an East Front view; it was taken in 1846, quite probably before this quilt was finished or maybe even begun. See United States Capitol Historical Society, *Washington Past and Present*, Washington, D.C., 1983, p. 18.

[6] William Rush Dunton, Jr., theorized extensively about Achsah Wilkins' quiltmaking activities in his book, *Old Quilts* (Catonsville, Md., 1946). Dena Katzenberg in *Baltimore Album Quilts* went further, connecting Mrs. Wilkins hypothetically to the Baltimore Album Quilts specifically. Mrs. Katzenberg's dates for Mrs. Wilkins are used here.

[7] Dena Katzenberg in *Baltimore Album Quilts* gives the birth/death dates for Achsah Wilkins as 1775–1854, making her about seventy-nine when she died, and seventy-three in 1848. Her dates for Mary Evans are 1829–1916, making her about eighty-seven when she died and nineteen in 1848.

[8] *We the People*, p. 31.

[9] Soundly defeated in the Battles of North Point and Fort McHenry, the British headed for Jamaica, then on to the Battle of New Orleans, General Andrew Jackson, and a bloodbath which ended the War: 2,036 British killed or wounded as against 8 Americans killed, 13 wounded.

[10] Francis Beirne, *The Amiable Baltimoreans*, Johns Hopkins University Press, Baltimore, 1951, p. 92.

[11] It may be this monument which was being represented in the basted City Springs block attributed to Mary Evans (*Volume I*, Photo 4). The Armistead Monument was erected "in a Gothic niche in the building at the rear of the old City Spring on Calvert Street, in Baltimore."

[12] Noting how frequently a red-fruited bough, often with birds, sometimes arboreal, sometimes as a heartshaped wreath, is in the same quilt with memorials to fallen war heroes, I'm inclined to think that cherries are intended. For, in the language of flowers, cherries mean Sweet Character and Good Deeds. The birds, often blue, mean Life of the Soul, and seem to imply that the hero will rest in heaven. The "cherry bough," if such it is, is in the Major Ringgold Quilt (carried aloft by bluebirds amidst a splendid array of fraternal symbols), the Sarah McIlwain Quilt, and quilt #3 in the Color Section. There, crossed keys (Keys to the heart or Love) fill the heartshaped wreath's center.

Laurel, also berried, is also appropriate, but does not have such serrate leaves and should be more bushlike than what seems clearly a tree over the monument in quilt #3. The fruit is sometimes shown quite graphically on cherry-long stems. Block C-1 in quilt #1 in the Color Section is a splendid example and block A-4 in the Shelburne's Major Ringgold Quilt is equally so. And the monuments in quilt #2? Might the floral crown hung on the lyre (Divine or Eternal Music) in block B-1 be a wreath of cherries and blossoms and thus convey the same import? If so, sprigs of these same are in the "Capitol" and the War of 1812, and possibly the George Washington Monument blocks. Birds (the eagle means Resurrection) are in all the building blocks except B-2.

[13] Might the gaslights have been a factor in the spread of two major conflagrations in Baltimore? The first began and ended Friday, July 25, 1873, the second started on a quiet Sunday morning, February 7, 1904. Of the 1904 fire, Frank Beirne writes in *The Amiable Baltimoreans*, "For more than thirty years the fire of 1873 held a conspicuous place in the annals of Baltimore catastrophes. Then in 1904, within a matter of hours, it was erased from memory by the fire which dwarfed all others and assumed the title of "The Fire." No Baltimorean since has had to ask which one" (p. 338). Although both fires occurred after the period when we believe the Album Quilts were made, they affect our study of these quilts, since many records—fraternal order membership records, family records, and church records—which might have proved useful were destroyed.

[14] Pericles' Funeral Oration on the occasion of the first casualties of the Peloponnesian War.

[15] Wendy Lavitt and Judith Weissman, *Labors of Love*, Knopf, New York, 1987, p. 140: "A huge variety of designs for Berlin work—14,000 of them were created between 1830 and 1840—provided a diversity of subjects and patterns. For pictures, biblical scenes, engravings, and well-known paintings like Leonardo da Vinci's Last Supper were popular, as were pastoral and medieval scenes. In the latter half of the century, large, garishly colored flowers, especially overblown roses, and exotic birds were also favorites."

[16] This monument seems to be represented in *Baltimore Album Quilts* (Figure 31) where it is inscribed "Ringgold"; in the Sarah McIlwain quilt, inscription illegible; in the "Major Ringgold quilt" (inscribed "Ringgold") in

An American Sampler; in the "Baltimore Album Quilt, 1848" (no inscription) shown in *Ho For California;* and in the Sarah Ann Lankford quilt (inscribed "Ringgold") in *Treasures of American Folk Art: from the Abby Aldrich Rockefeller Folk Art Center.* Two other very different looking monuments or tombs are shown in *Old Quilts,* in Plate 15 (no inscription) and in Plate 3 (with "Watson" and "1846" appliquéd above it).

[17] Arthur Schlesinger, editor, *The Almanac of American History,* Putnam, New York, 1983, p. 251. The battle must have been fierce, one report contending that the Americans lost 39 men with 83 wounded while Mexico's losses were even higher: 262 dead, 35 wounded, with 150 others captured.

[18] James McSherry, *History of Maryland,* Baltimore Book Company, Baltimore, Md., 1904, p. 333.

[19] *Ibid.,* 334.

[20] *Ibid.,* 333.

[21] *Ibid.,* p. 336.

[22] The accession notations which accompanied this quilt's photo from the St. Louis Museum of Art were most helpful. Though nothing seems to have been conveyed about its early provenance, three examinations of these inscriptions are recorded and transcribed: the first in 1973; a second revision done on May 6, 1981; and a third from an examination of blocks C-2 and D-2 by Kristan McKinsey. Her revision has been incorporated here with the 1981 one, each successive reading eliminating some illegibility, having deciphered incrementally more of these inscriptions. The sum of the effort witnesses the difficulty of the task.

"DEATH OF MAJOR RINGGOLD, OF THE FLYING ARTILLERY, AT THE BATTLE OF PALO ALTO, MAY 8, 1846." *Major Samuel Ringgold was one of Baltimore's best-loved heroes of the war for Texas independence, the Mexican-American War. Here shown shot through both legs by a cannon ball, his honor and altruism were legendary. History notes that a contingent of Marylanders embarked "in the Fall" to retrieve his body which later lay in state in the Merchant's Exchange in Baltimore in December of that year. Multiple Album quiltmakers stitched a monument and possibly other memorials to him and fellow Baltimorean Colonel William Watson, who fell just four months after Ringgold. (Photo courtesy Library of Congress)*

Part Two: The Patterns

The patterns that follow are given on one, two, and four pages. The pattern transfer method depends on the number of pages and is explained in detail in *Volume I* in Part One: Getting Started. Patterns are presented on the outside corner of each page for easy tracing. When I have had to make up a name for a pattern, I note this with an asterisk (*). Symbolic meanings given for the appliqué motifs were taken from *Spoken Without a Word*.

PATTERN #1: "Fleur-de-Lis Medallion I"*

Type: Classic "Baltimore" (from quilt inscribed "1844" and "Baltimore.")

To make this block, refer to *Volume I*, Lessons 1 or 2.

The fleur-de-lis was so very popular a motif that it was often included as a secondary motif in other more complex patterns. This version, with four units forming a medallion center, must have taken a great stretch of the imagination to compose. But since its open center offered an attractive frame for an inscription, it too was repeated and was itself subject to creative adaptations.

Finely appliquéd by Gerri Rathbun, John Wesley's "Rule of Conduct" has been inscribed in this block's center: "Do all the good you can, By all the means you can, In all the ways you can, In all the places you can, At all the times you can, To all the people you can, As long as ever you can." This injunction by the founder of Methodism appeals both

continued on page 172

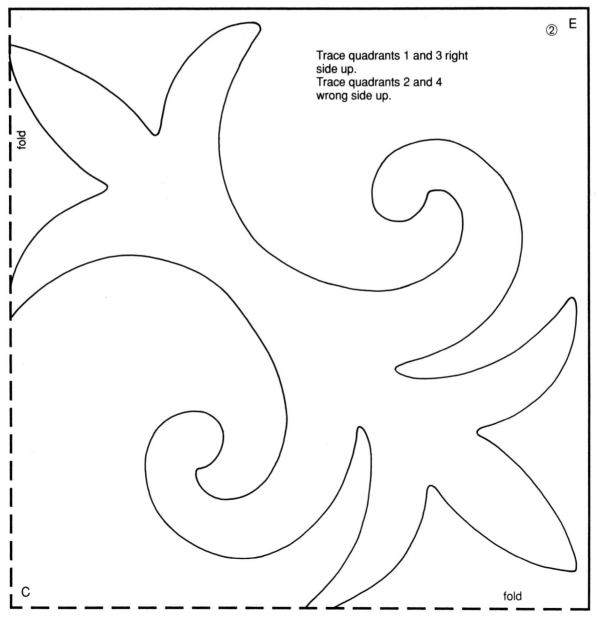

Trace quadrants 1 and 3 right side up.
Trace quadrants 2 and 4 wrong side up.

PATTERN #6: "Hearts and Swans I and II"*

Type: "Beyond"

To make this block, refer to *Volume I*, Lesson 1 or 2.

I was recently asked to teach appliqué at "Quilt Expo Europa 1990" in Odense, Denmark, the home of Hans Christian Andersen. This charming writer shared the same passion for papercuts as is reflected in the classic Album quilts. Determined to teach appliqué on a Hans Christian Andersen theme, I designed a number of blocks, including "Hearts and Swans." Because a circular red papercut makes an excellent classic Album Quilt center block, Mary Wise Miller made Version II, reduced to allow room for the inscription. Equally challenged, Georganna Clark made Version I.

Andersen may simply have been using favorite symbols without much thought to their meaning, though as a Victorian man of letters, he would have understood their

continued on page 172

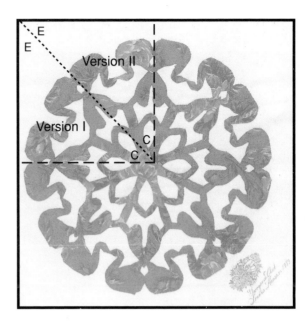

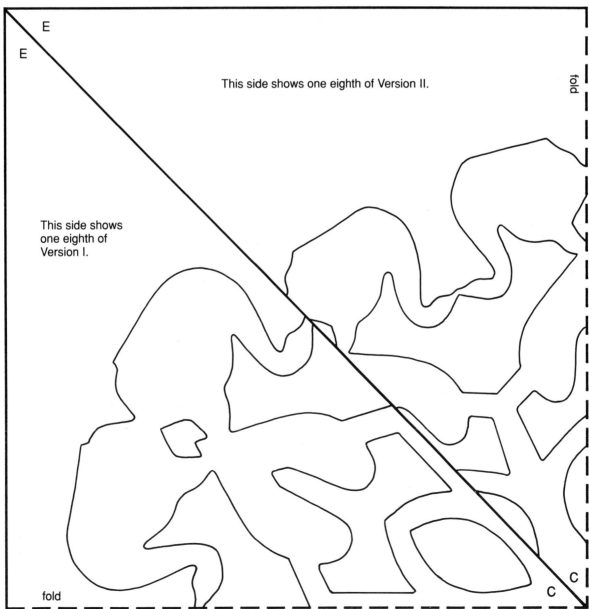

E

E

This side shows one eighth of Version II.

This side shows one eighth of Version I.

fold

fold

C

C

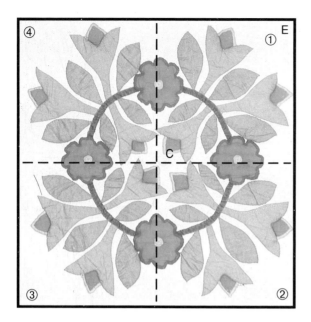

PATTERN #7: "Rose of Sharon II"

Type: Classic "Baltimore"

To make this block, refer to *Volume I*, Lessons 1 or 2, and 5 or 10.

Detail: Quilt #1 in the Color Section.

Rose of Sharon I appears, unnumbered, in *Spoken Without a Word;* hence this is Version II. They are basically the same block, but this time the wreath has a lushly charming fullness to it. The pattern is drawn so it can be sewn as shown in separate unit appliqué or the green portions may be done by cutwork appliqué from one fabric. I have always called this the Rose of Sharon though Cuesta Benberry, who is very knowledgeable about such things, calls it a President's Wreath.

PATTERN #8: "Folk Art Flower Wheel"*

Type: Classic "Baltimore"

To make this block, refer to *Volume I*, Lesson 5. See also Appendix I in this book.

Detail: Quilt #4 in the Color Section.

This charming pattern of flowers around a cutwork wheel has a strong German, or "Pennsylvania Dutch" aspect ("Dutch" comes from *Deutsch,* i.e., Pennsylvania German). This particular stylization, with the inlaid flowers, simple shapes, and bold clear colors (some of rainbow fabric shading from light to dark) seems to be a design style which constitutes a minor and repeated theme in the classic Baltimore Album Quilts. See also Pattern #34, and, in quilt #3 in the Color Section, blocks C-5, D-5, and possibly even B-3 and D-1.

continued on page 172

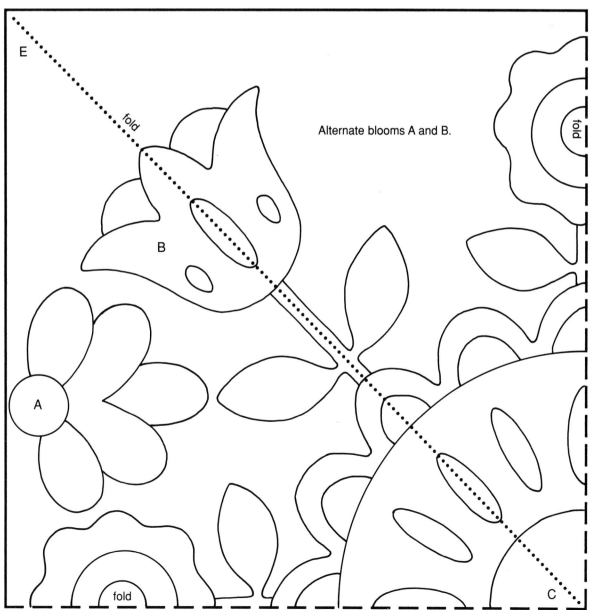

Alternate blooms A and B.

PATTERN #9: "Hearts and Tulips"*

Type: Classic "Baltimore"

To make this block, refer to *Volume I*, Lessons 3 and 5.

Detail: *Volume I*, quilt #6.

This block is so "modern" that it could have been designed today. It seems, however, to have originated in the mid-nineteenth century in the environs of Baltimore. Dramatic in red and green, its symbolic meaning is equally exuberant: tulips suggest a Declaration of Love, and hearts mean Love or Devotion. One could play this possible symbolic intent out a bit further, imputing to the ring of hearts the circle's meaning of Never-ending, or Eternal, Love. Then again, one can't be absolutely sure these are meant to be tulips!

We might guess that this was a Pennsylvania Dutch pattern, the style we most think of as "folk art." In fact this

continued on page 172

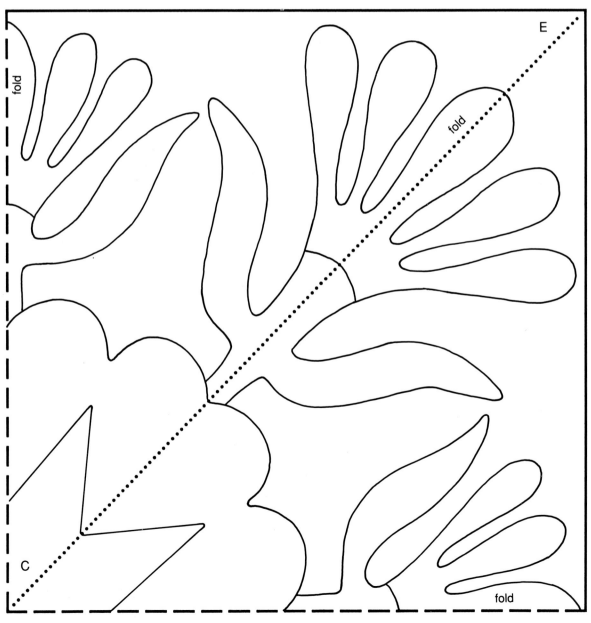

PATTERN #10: "Red Vases and Red Flowers"*

Type: "Beyond"

To make this block, refer to *Volume I*, Lesson 5.

Detail: *Volume I*, quilt #6. Design from Montgomery County, Maryland, inscribed in part, "Mary, Remember me/William Thomas Johnson/1851." Original quilt in the collection of the DAR Museum, Washington, D.C.

This is block B-5 from quilt #6 in *Volume I*. Done there in reverse appliqué, it was awkward to sew from the off-white down to two continguate colors, the red and the green. Perhaps this explains why the reverse appliqué on classic Album Quilts seems always to be the background fabric, cut and turned back to reveal just one single color or fabric, an approach which would work better.

What flower might this be? Dr. Dunton refers to a wreath of similar-looking flowers in the Samuel Williams

continued on page 172

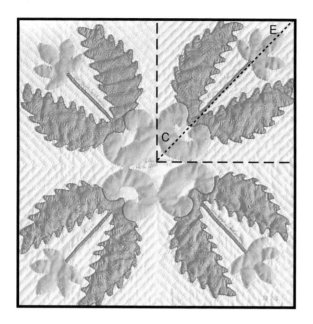

PATTERN #11: "Victorian Favorite"*

Type: Classic "Baltimore"

To make this block, refer to *Volume I*, Lesson 5.

Detail: *Volume I*, quilt #6.

This pattern abounds in the classic appliqué Album Quilts. One can also see this particular blossom in the quilting pattern of the occasional Pennsylvania appliqué quilt of the period. The block's center has a version of an almost Ionic motif which reads as a vase. In Freemasonry, which permeated the American decorative arts of the eighteenth to middle-nineteenth century, the Ionic order symbolizes Wisdom. In addition, acanthus leaves mean Admiring of the Fine Arts, also a Masonic virtue. However, art historian Alan Gowans cautions, "Masonry could not have been more than a supporting thread in the over-all Victorian esthetic." The Album quiltmakers,

continued on page 172

PATTERN #12: "Christmas Cactus I"*

Type: Classic "Baltimore"

To make this block, refer to *Volume I*, Lessons 1 or 2, and 5.

Detail: *Volume I*, quilt #6.

The Christmas cactus seems to have been a relatively oft-repeated block in the classic Album Quilts but this one seems the most graceful, elegant, and realistic.

The plant, first hybridized in the 1840s by William Buckley, an English gardener, surely seems additional proof that the early Album quiltmakers were very current on their natural history, and took "rational pleasure" in recording the latest botanical imports in their quilts. Not only have their quilts survived, but so have some of these early hybrids as well. "It is not uncommon for a Christmas cactus nurtured in the nineteenth century to survive several generations," writes Judith Hillstrom in her

continued on page 173

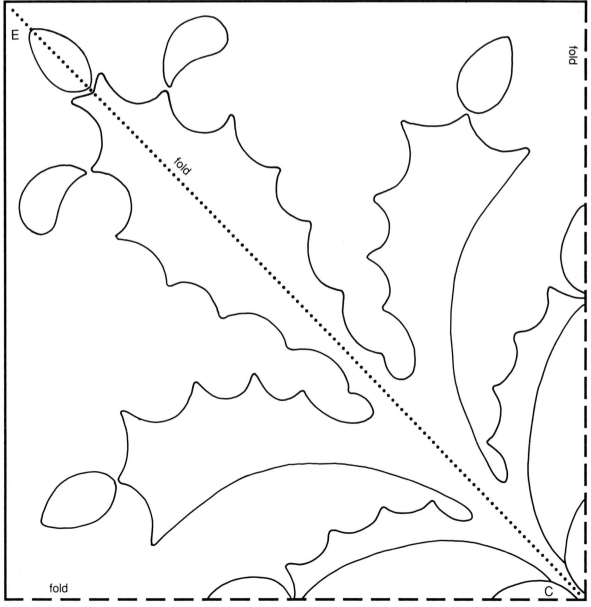

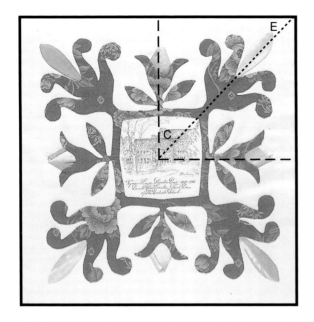

PATTERN #13 "Fleur-de-Lis with Rosebuds III"*

Type: "Beyond"

To make this block, refer to *Volume I*, Lessons 1 or 2, and 6.

This pattern is based on a block from a quilt in the Numsen family. The pattern shows that version although it's been taken a bit "beyond" by the inclusion of folded 3½"-diameter circle rosebuds from Lesson 6. With its bold two-color fleurs-de-lis and enlarged framelike center, it is a particularly graceful and appealing version of the block which recurs in many forms in these classic quilts. Why might this square wreath (symbolizing Earthly Matters), with fleurs-de-lis (see the notes to Pattern #2), and rosebuds (Beauty, Purity, Youth) or as a rose, Love, have been so popular? Was it for its meaning? Did it have a meaning as yet unfathomed? Or did avid pattern collectors simply want the variety of a square wreath added to their Albums?

continued on page 173

PATTERN #14: "Fleur-de-Lis with Rosebuds IV"*

Type: "Beyond"

To make this block, refer to *Volume I*, Lessons 1 or 2, and 6.

This is one of my original versions of the popular fleur-de-lis and rosebud block. Why design more of this block motif when there are already so many? First, I was drawn back to these blocks by Version III (Pattern #13) which had a wonderfully open square center. That open center called to me as an ideal place to make this into a picture block, blocks that portray people, buildings, or places (discussed in detail in *Volume II*). Once I'd inked two Version III blocks with scenes, I came back to Pattern #10, Version II (in *Volume I*), and saw that by changing its interior, one could make a nice square on-point central medallion picture frame. Or one could make a slightly less open frame by adding back in the rosebuds. There are three different size circles used in this block to make

continued on page 173

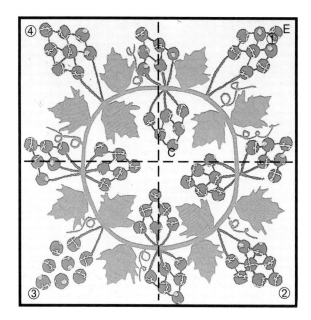

PATTERN #15: "Grapevine Wreath II"

Type: Baltimore-style

To make this block, refer to *Volume I*, Lessons 1 or 2, and 9.

Detail: Quilt #1 in the Color Section.

This highly stylized grapevine intrigued me with its very realistic leaves and its geometric Chinese-checker-like grape pattern. This precise grapebunch layout occurs elsewhere in these quilts, but infrequently. Excited, I imagined a seaman returning from the Orient, his clipper ship intently watched for from a widow's walk, his gift to his waiting Baltimore quiltmaking bride, a game of Chinese checkers. Needless to say, I was disappointed to find that Chinese checkers is a modern pasttime, being a 1930s version of the game "Halma."

The grape may quite possibly be the most common fruit in the Baltimore Album Quilts. These are largely Christian

continued on page 173

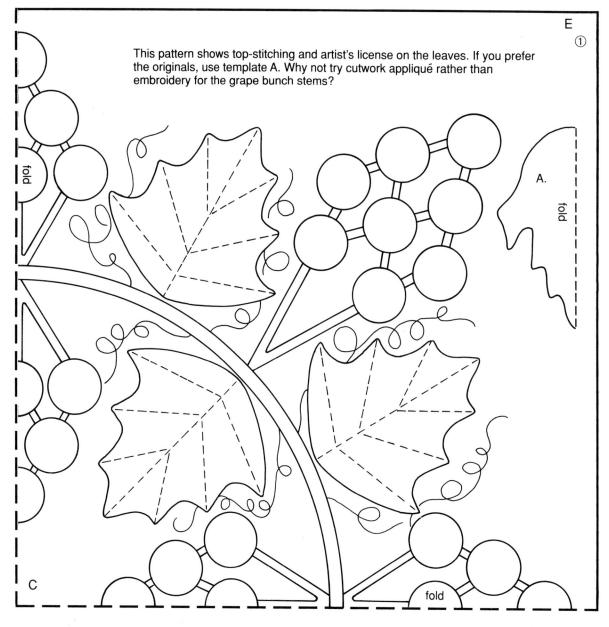

This pattern shows top-stitching and artist's license on the leaves. If you prefer the originals, use template A. Why not try cutwork appliqué rather than embroidery for the grape bunch stems?

PATTERN #16: "Strawberry Wreath II"*

Type: Baltimore-style

To make this block, refer to *Volume I*, Lessons 5 and 9.

Detail: Quilt #1 in the Color Section.

A classic-style Album Quilt block, this Strawberry Wreath is embellished with embroidery. Being circular, the wreath could intend Eternal Things and its strawberries Esteem and Love, or Intoxication and Delight. The strawberry leaves symbolize Completion and Perfection.

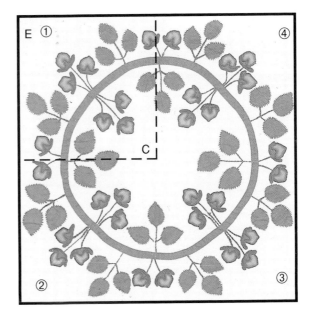

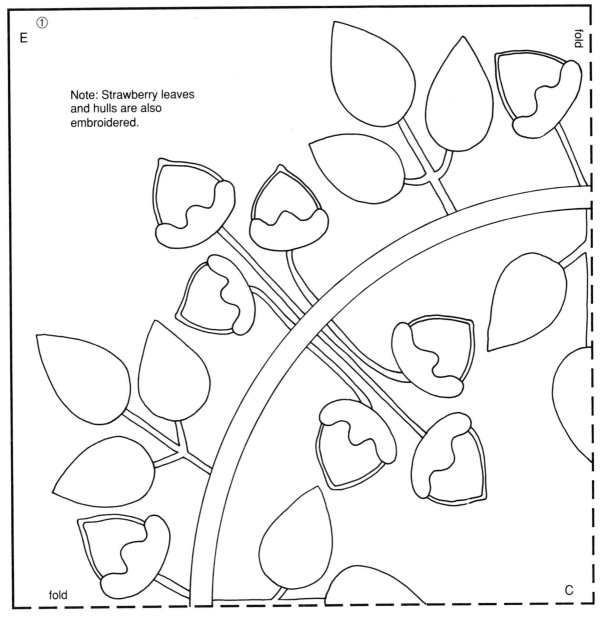

Note: Strawberry leaves and hulls are also embroidered.

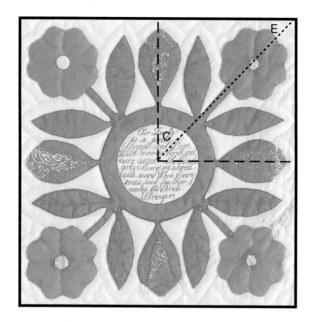

PATTERN #17: "Rose of Sharon III"*

Type: Classic "Baltimore"

To make this block, refer to *Volume I*, Lessons 1 or 2, 5 or 10.

Detail: *Volume I*, quilt #7.

This particular Rose Wreath I have seen only on mid-nineteenth-century Maryland Album Quilts. Intrigued by its simplicity, I decided to add intricacy to an otherwise plain block so I inked much of it to look like engraving. One flower I left unembellished so you can see the difference the inking has made. See Lessons 3 and 7 (*Volume I*) for instructions on writing and drawing on your block.

I have called this a Rose of Sharon, though others may know it differently. The Rose of Sharon harkens back to its Biblical reference in the Song of Solomon and symbolizes Wedded Love.

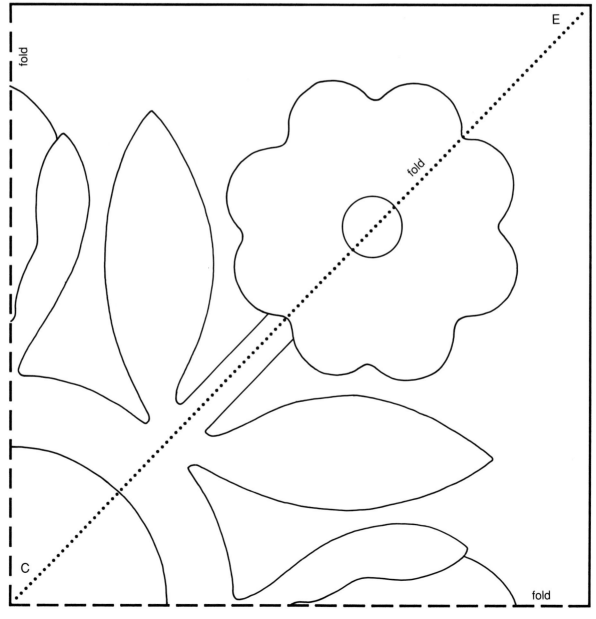

PATTERN #18: "Circular Sprays of Flowers"*

Type: Baltimore-style

To make this block, refer to *Volume I*, Lessons 1 or 2, 5 or 10.

Detail: Quilt #1 in the Color Section.

This is a charming block and refreshingly easy to make! Perhaps there was a real competition going on, if only within a given quiltmaker's breast, to come up with as many conceivable ways to show sprays of flowers as possible: in baskets, vases, cornucopias; set in square, round, lyre, or heart-shaped wreaths, and in single sprays or double or tied as bouquets. This charming way of showing a wreath seems truly unique.

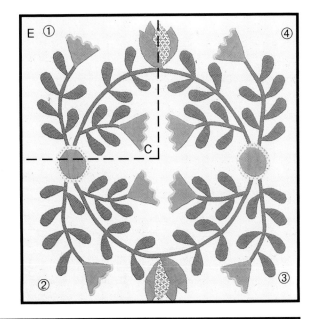

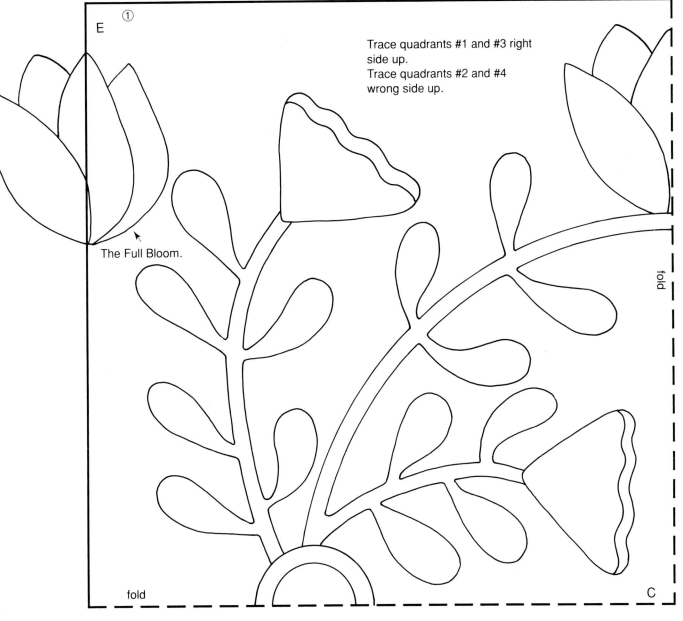

Trace quadrants #1 and #3 right side up.
Trace quadrants #2 and #4 wrong side up.

The Full Bloom.

fold

fold

E ①

C

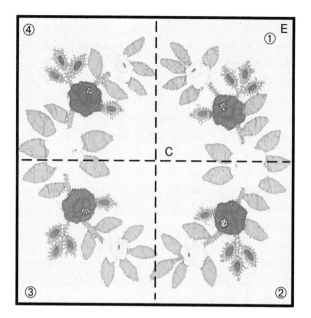

PATTERN #19: "Broken Wreath of Roses"*

Type: Classic "Baltimore"

To make this block, refer to *Volume I*, Lessons 5, 7, 9, or 10. See also Appendix I in this book.

Detail: Quilt #3 in the Color Section.

Another pattern design and construction theme that runs through the classic Baltimore Album Quilts is the stuffed and heavily embroidered one shown by this graceful block. Quite similar is Pattern #20, the "Wreath of Roses." While that is a whole wreath, this is actually a two-half-circle wreath, a rare variation of the more common broken wreath which is broken only at the top. Bright in Victoria green and Turkey red with contrasting white roses, this block entices the quiltmaker who loves the fancywork of embroidered embellishments. The roses are padded and back-stitch quilted to petaled effect, and the

continued on page 173

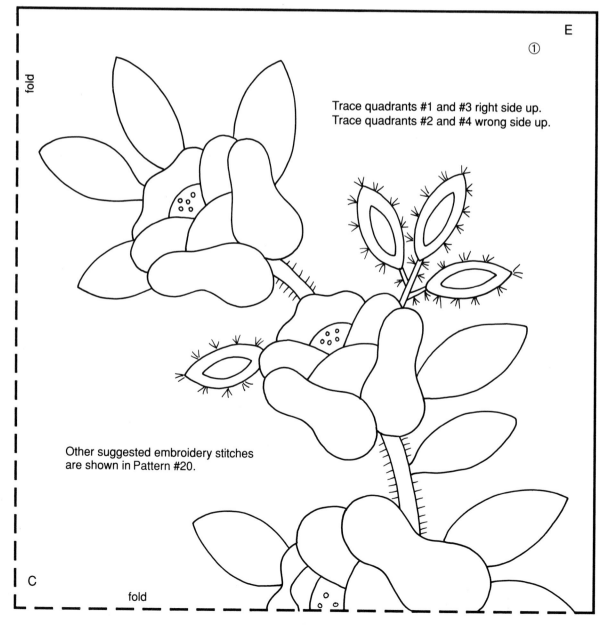

E

①

Trace quadrants #1 and #3 right side up.
Trace quadrants #2 and #4 wrong side up.

Other suggested embroidery stitches
are shown in Pattern #20.

fold

C

fold

PATTERN #20: "Wreath of Roses"*

Type: Classic "Baltimore"

To make this block, refer to *Volume I*, Lessons 5, 7, and 9. See also Appendix I in this volume.

Detail: Quilt #3 in the Color Section.

Dr. Dunton, recording this quilt in *Old Quilts* (p. 22), provides his usual complete description: "Wreath of Roses. Leaves are of the 3-2 type. (Three outside, two inside between the roses.) Four are white and four red. All are padded and shaded with silk. The wool stitching of the red and white buds and outlining the white roses is light blue. All roses have yellow wool pistils, leaves of black on green of tiny black diamonds (1½ x 3½ mm.) with a small yellow dot in the centre of each. Diamonds are 5 mm. apart diagonally in rows. Inserted in the centre of the block is a pen and ink drawing of a hummingbird

continued on page 173

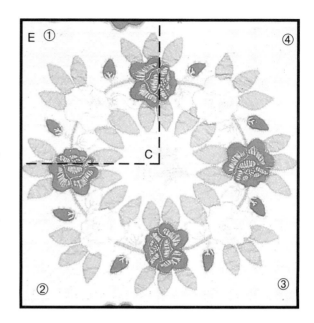

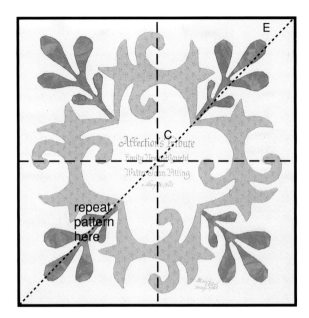

PATTERN #21 "Fleur-de-Lis Medallion II*

Type: Classic "Baltimore"

To make this block, refer to *Volume I*, Lessons 1 or 2, 5 or 10.

One specific reason for the popular inclusion of the fleur-de-lis could be what can be called none other than love for the gallant Marquis de Lafayette, a hero of grand proportions in the early history of this country.

Rousseauian romantic idealism spurred on young Marie Joseph Paul, Marquis de Lafayette (1757–1834) to support the American Revolutionary cause. If fame were also a motive, fortune was not, for he served as an unsalaried volunteer and eventually spent some $200,000 of his own for the American cause. Commissioned as a major general, he was a skilled and able leader as well as a close, supportive friend to General Washington. On leave to France, he did much to assist the American cause. Back in America, he so aided in the defense of

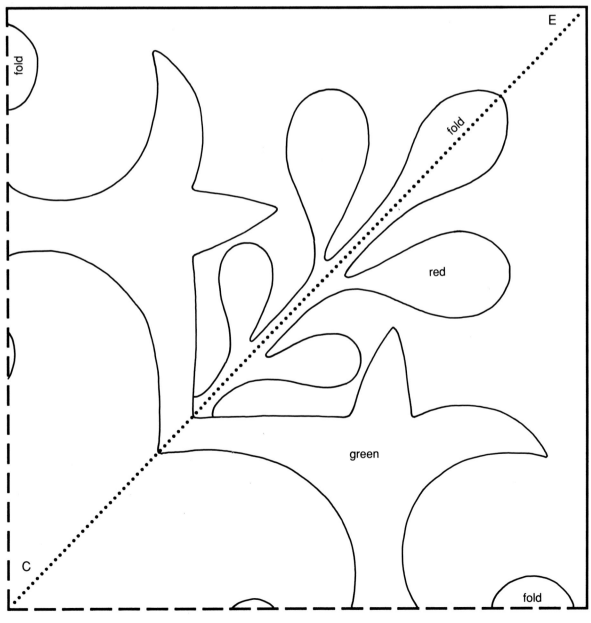

PATTERN #21 "Fleur-de-Lis Medallion II*

Second Page

Richmond that when he again returned to France he had earned considerable fame and was greeted with adulation. With wild enthusiam, the American populace welcomed him back on his 1784 visit to the United States. The citizens of Maryland bestowed permanent citizenship upon him, making him one of their own.

Though sympathetic with the ideals of the French Revolution, when it came, his aristocratic birth caused him to be imprisoned for five years and robbed of his estates. Realizing that America's loyal friend was now himself in need, Congress paid Lafayette his back $24,424 brigadier-general's pay and eventually granted land in Louisiana to him.

In the spring of 1781, the "dashing young Marquis de Lafayette" had ridden into Baltimore, leading his troops "on the way South and stopped for the night. The good

continued on page 173

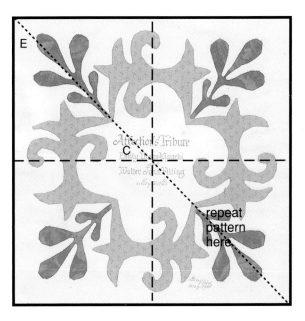

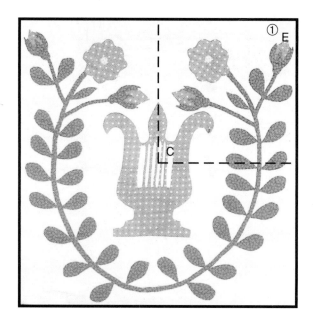

PATTERN #22: "Rose Lyre II"*

Type: Baltimore-style

To make this block, refer to *Volume I,* Lessons 1 or 2, or 5.

Detail: Quilt #1 in the Color Section.

Pretty, easy to make, and imbued with sweetly sentimental symbolism, this block may be irresistible. "Sure as the grape grows on the vine/So sure you are my valentine/The rose is red the violet blue/Lilies are fair and so are you."[8] Who does not understand a gift of flowers to be a Token of Affection? From birth, to marriage, to death, we mark the moment with flowers.

Greek and Roman myths tell love stories for almost every kind of flower, but especially for the rose, the symbol of Love. The rose was sacred to Venus, Roman goddess of spring, bloom, and beauty, who was later identified with the Greek Aphrodite as the goddess of love. One myth connects the rose to Cupid, telling that he spilled nectar on

PATTERN #22: "Rose Lyre II"*

Second Page

the ground and it bubbled back up in the form of roses. Explaining nature, as myths do, we are told how the rose got its thorns: Opening only to the kiss of Zephyr, the soft West wind, the rose was kissed one day by amorous Cupid. A bee, trapped inside, stung him. Angry, Venus had Cupid thread the bees on his bowstring: their stings she planted along the stem of the rose where, ever since, they remain as thorns.

All roses mean Love: "And the white rose breathes of love;/O, the red rose is a falcon,/and the white rose is a dove."[9] This love need not be romantic love. And thus we see roses on monument blocks for fallen war heroes such as that in quilt #3 in the Color Section. In fact this block, too, could be an "in memoriam" block with the lyre meaning Eternal Music. Or it could mean, may our [your] love last forever, a heartfelt wish of love!

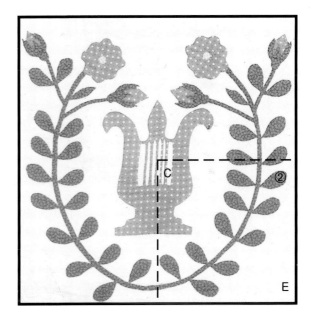

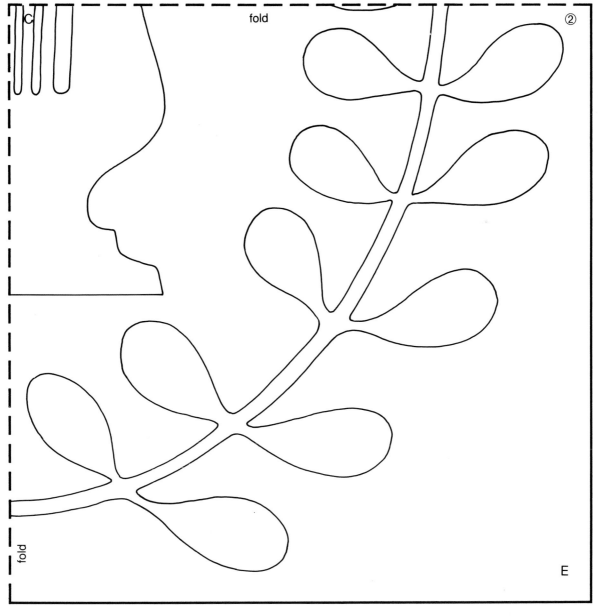

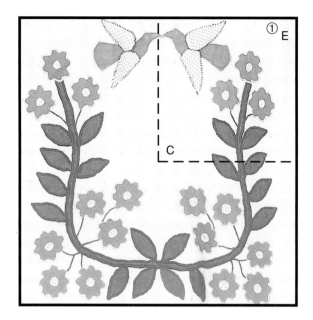

PATTERN #23: "Redbird Lyre"*

Type: Baltimore-style

To make this block, refer to *Volume I*, Lessons 1 or 2, and 5.

Detail: Quilt #1 in the Color Section.

Virginia Piland, an extraordinary contemporary quilt-maker, always records on a block if it was sewn on a holiday. This, then is a block to be begun on Valentine's Day, and, drawing heavily on Edna Barth's knowledge,[10] here's why. Perhaps because several species mate in February, Medieval man believed all birds chose their mate on St. Valentine's Day: "For this was on St. Valentine's Day/When every fowl cometh to choose his mate."[11] And, since Noah and the flood, doves had served as messengers, coming in classical times to be connected to Venus and other deities of love. Being of the pigeon family, doves mate for life, are gentle, and murmur comfortingly with their billing and cooing, and so

Note: the lyre stem and leaves are also embroidered in what appears to be button hole or whipped satin stitch.

PATTERN #23: "Redbird Lyre"*

Second Page

prove a happy choice as the bird of love. These doves, on wing above the lyre, which speaks of Divine Music, would seem to sing of Eternal Love. At least, then, we should let them sing of Valentines!

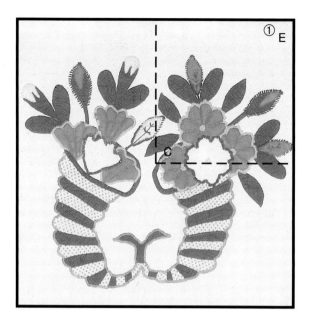

PATTERN #24: "Rose Cornucopias"*

Type: Baltimore-style

To make this block, refer to *Volume I*, Lessons 5, 9, or 10.

Detail: Quilt #1 in the Color Section.

If you covet cornucopias for your quilt, this is our simplest rendition yet, though to keep it in the moderately easy category, one would have to side-step the exquisite, but time-consuming embroidery. Note that in the original, pursuing what seems to have been a Victorian aesthetic ideal of asymmetry, each horn holds differently rendered blooms. A cornucopia speaks of Abundance, roses of Love. Were I a betting woman, I'd say our block's subject is love, sweet love, and plenty of it!

Cornucopias were a popular Victorian decorative motif, bespeaking the earth's plenty. Edna Barth in *Turkeys, Pilgrims, and Indian Corn* tells us that the cornucopia motif goes back at least to classical Greece. "The

PATTERN #24: "Rose Cornucopias"*

Second Page

Greeks had several myths about cornucopia, their name for the horn of plenty. One of these tells of Amalthea, a goat who suckled the infant god Zeus. Once Amalthea broke off one of her horns. Filling it with fruits and flowers, she gave it to Zeus. To show his gratitude, Zeus later set the goat's image in the sky as the constellation Capricorn. In another myth, Amalthea was a nymph who raised Zeus on goat's milk. The grateful young god broke off the goat's horn and gave it to his kind foster mother. This horn of plenty would supply her an abundance of whatever she wanted."[12] Clearly gratitude for abundance is also symbolized by the cornucopia motif from ancient harvest festivals to our own Thanksgiving.

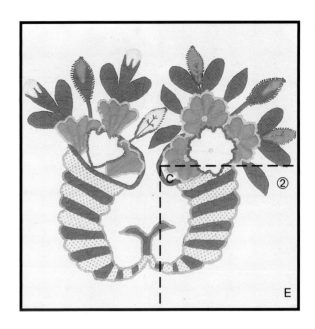

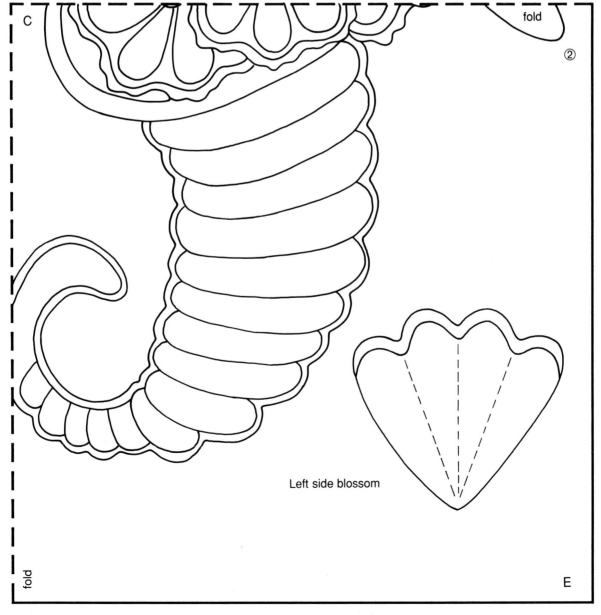

Left side blossom

PATTERN #25: "Lyre with Laurel Sprays I"*

Type: Classic "Baltimore"

To make this block, refer to *Volume I*, Lessons 1 or 2, 5, or 10.

Detail: *Volume I*, quilt #4, the classic 1846–47 Baltimore Album Quilt "made for Angeline Hoffman."

This is a particularly successful and endearing version of a simplified lyre block. Lyres are among the most frequently found motifs in these classic quilts. Symbolizing All Music in Honor of God, and Eternal Music, the lyre carries connotations of eternity and things everlasting. Thus, hypothetically, it could mean "in memoriam" in some blocks. Add laurel (for Success, Renown, Victory) to the lyre and this motif might read Eternal Renown, or Victory in Eternity, even Eternal Honor and Devotion. Perhaps the intent was so undeniably good that one did not have to specify!

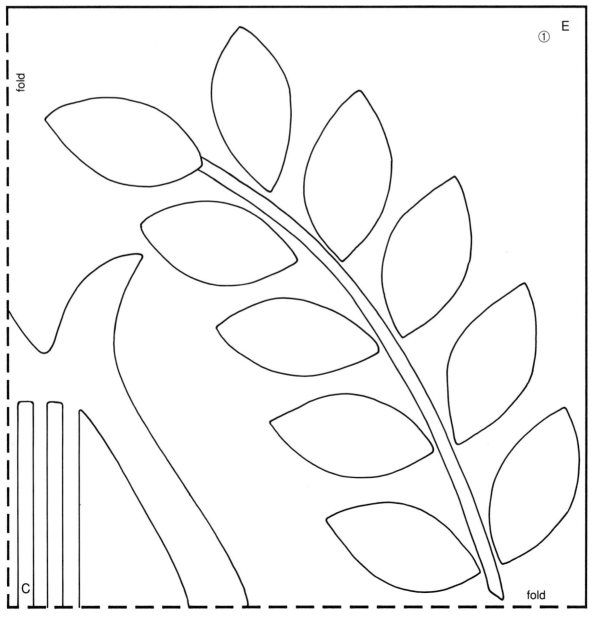

PATTERN #25: "Lyre with Laurel Sprays I"*

Second Page

This heart-decorated lyre seems to be framed by the classic green leaf/red leaf stylization of laurel sprays. Here, though, rather than the red leaves coming at the tips of the sprays, they line one side. All the red on this block could be done by cutwork appliqué (*Volume I*, Lesson 1 or 2); then the green could be added by separate unit appliqué (Appendix I in this book).

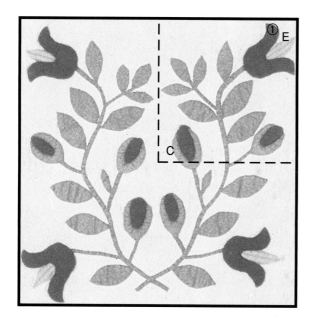

PATTERN #26: "Crossed Sprays of Flowers"*

Type: Classic "Baltimore"

To make this block, refer to *Volume I*, Lessons 1 or 2, 5, or 10.

Detail: Quilt #3 in the Color Section.

This is a charming, simple arrangement of a gracefully meandering stem, which, mirrored, supports four stuffed red and yellow tulips, six black-edged red buds, and numerous leaves of varied sizes. Although crossed floral sprays are common in the Album Quilts, this particular version is unusual, perhaps unique. Done by cutwork appliqué, it is relatively quick and easy.

PATTERN #26: "Crossed Sprays of Flowers"*

Second Page

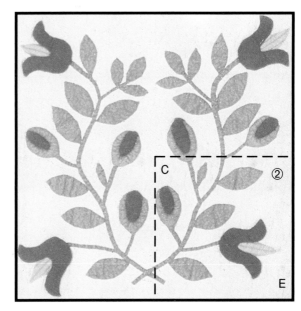

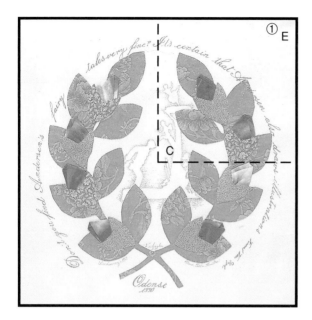

PATTERN #27: "Roses for Hans Christian Andersen"*

Type: "Beyond"

To make this block, refer to *Volume I*, Lessons 1 or 2, and 6.

Here is another block designed for the Odense Album Quilt, mentioned in the notes to Pattern #6. Who would think this block was quick and easy? Perhaps that's part of its beauty, for the cutwork appliqué leaf/stem framework has been simplified to the utmost with soft outward points and just a few inward points. The folded circle roses are so simple, too, but happily that's your secret! This is an elegant choice to make as a gift, perhaps in a frame to note some special occasion. Or perhaps your gift will be to a Friendship Album in classic Baltimore tradition.

PATTERN #27: "Roses for Hans Christian Andersen"*

Second Page

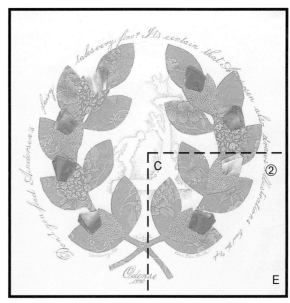

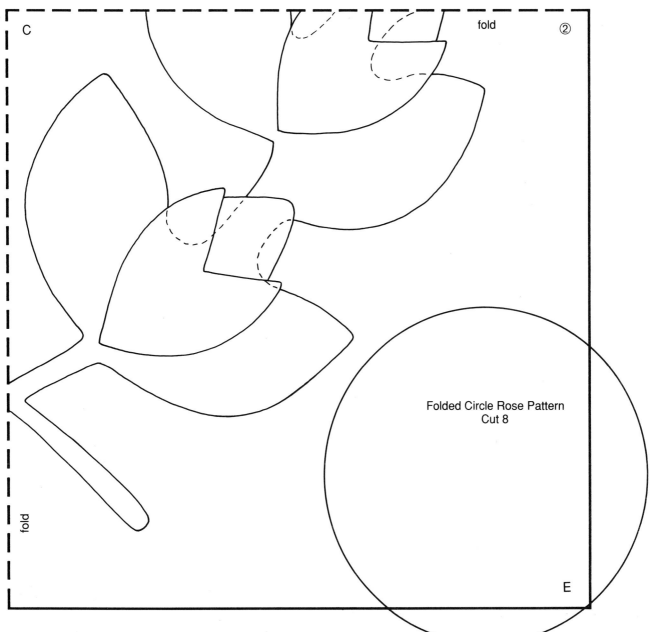

C

fold   ②

Folded Circle Rose Pattern
Cut 8

fold

E

PATTERN #28: "Grapevine Lyre Wreath"*

Type: "Beyond"

To make this block, refer to *Volume I*, Lesson 9 or 10.

Framing a Hans Christian Andersen papercut in silhouette, this is another of my designs from the Odense Album Quilt, mentioned in the notes to Pattern #6. Tie-dyed fabric from Marty Lawrence and New York Beauty imitates the rainbow fabric of old Baltimore and adds greatly to this block. A tour de force of superfine stems and perfect grapes!

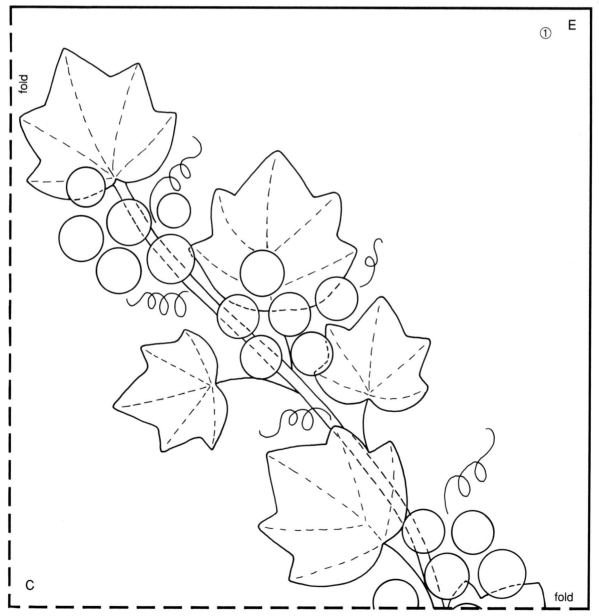

PATTERN #28: "Grapevine Lyre Wreath"*

Second Page

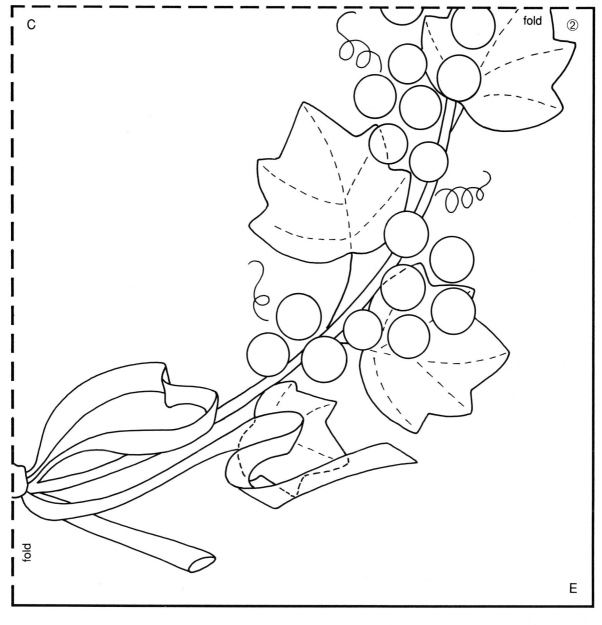

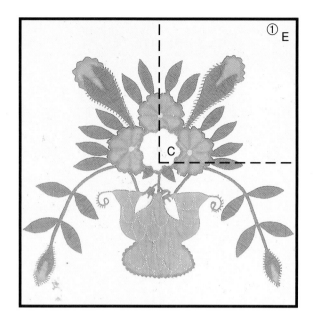

PATTERN #29: "Vase of Full-Blown Roses IV"*

Type: Classic "Baltimore"

To make this block, refer to *Volume I*, Lessons 5, 9, or 10. See also Appendix I in this book.

Detail: Quilt #1 in the Color Section.

The vase of full-blown roses was often repeated in delightful variety. The combination of three red and one white rose seems to have been a favorite, whether for aesthetic or symbolic reasons. The language of flowers offers little information on that score, except to suggest that a white rose means Purity or "I am worthy of you." A vase of full-blown roses means a Token of Gratitude. Elegantly embroidered, this block is a needlework gem. The vase is top-stitched in the clamshell pattern. To date, it seems to be a one-of-a-kind rendition of this block, placed in a position of pride and honor at the center of the quilt.

PATTERN #29: "Vase of Full-Blown Roses IV"*

Second Page

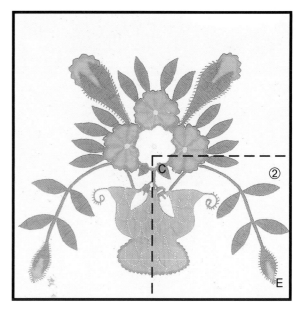

C

fold

②

fold

Buds and
vase handles have
white wool or cotton
whip stitch overcasting
one or more edges.

E

PATTERN #30: "Vase with Fruits and Flowers"*

Type: Classic "Baltimore"

To make this block, refer to *Volume I*, Lessons 5, 9, or 10. See also Appendix I in this book.

Detail: Quilt #1 in the Color Section.

Wild and wonderful, this block seems filled with symbolism—but the secret's not out yet. With careful precision, the clusters of four circles—two red, two yellow—proceed around the bouquet, and lest you wonder if they be another fruit, the cherries dangle on long stems. The cherries mean Sweet Character, Good Deeds. If "cherry twins," they mean Love's Charms and are a good luck symbol. Roses mean Love, that much is known. If you decode this pretty presentation of posies, please pass the poem along! For efficiency, we have shown this as a two-page pattern, where its asymmetry would otherwise

PATTERN #30: "Vase with Fruits and Flowers"*

Second Page

require four. All the elements are here, however, and by mixing leaves and buds a bit, you can capture the original again.

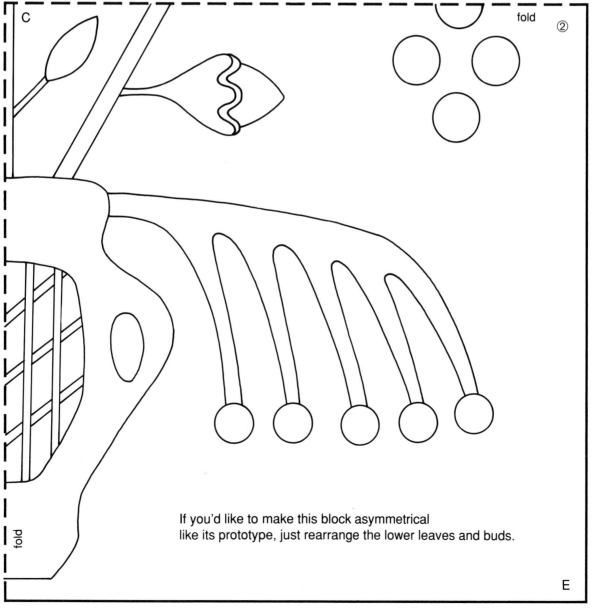

If you'd like to make this block asymmetrical
like its prototype, just rearrange the lower leaves and buds.

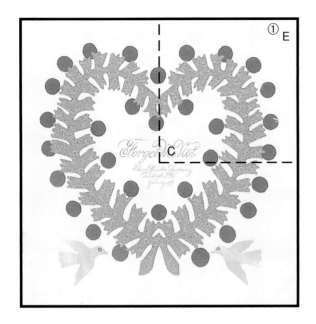

PATTERN #31: "Cherry Wreath with Bluebirds I and II"*

Type: Classic "Baltimore"

To make this block, refer to *Volume I*, Lessons 1 or 2, 5, and 9.

Wreathed hearts are among the most often repeated of the classic Album Quilt blocks. There are variations in both the style of the vine-wreathed hearts and in the motifs which sometimes accompany them; crossed keys (Keys to the Heart, Love), birds (Life of the Soul), kissing "lovebirds" (actually small parrots), hearts paired (True Love), and arrow-pierced hearts (Lovestruck or Repentance) are among these. Vine-wreathed hearts are both beautiful and imbued with symbolic meaning. Hearts mean Love, Devotion, Charity, or, to Scandinavians, Good Luck. The vine, if a grapevine, carries the meaning for Christians of the Church. (See Pattern #15 for

continued on page 173

PATTERN #31: "Cherry Wreath with Bluebirds I and II"*

Second Page

Version II

For Version II, place the centerfold of the heart on the diagonal centerfold of the fabric.

Friendship's Offering

Version I

Forget Me Not

fold

C

fold

②

E

E

PATTERN #32: "Diagonal Floral Spray I"*
(Shown with Pattern #33)

Type: Classic "Baltimore"

To make this block, refer to *Volume I*, Lessons 1 or 2, 5, and 9. See also Appendix I in this book.

Detail: Quilt #1 in the Color Section. A simpler version is block E-5 in the 1846–47 quilt in *Volume I*, quilt #4, "made for Angeline Hoffman."

Of course, one cannot prove beyond a doubt if a specific flower was intended in this block's prototype. However, these flowers look very much like peonies. Another version of the peony may be seen as the central medallion and border motif in quilts #7 and #8 in *Volume I*. Referring to our floral vocabulary, the peony symbolizes Healing and is thus a benevolent symbol to include in an Album Quilt.

These diagonal sprays occur with some frequency in the Baltimore Album Quilts. It occurred to me that this

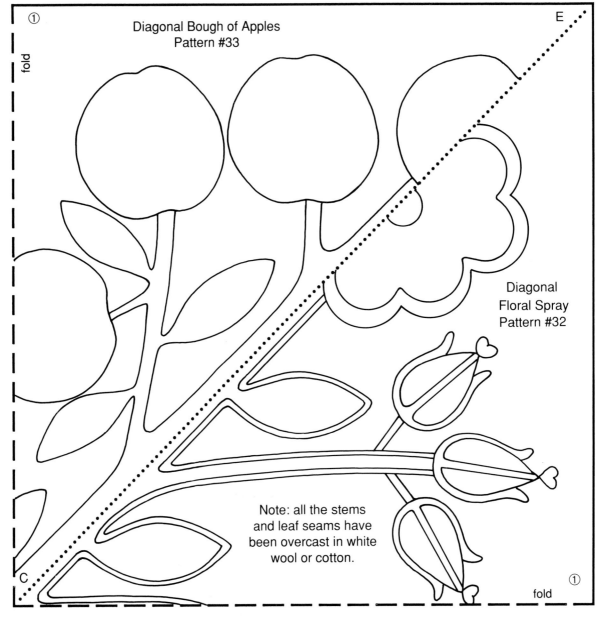

Diagonal Bough of Apples
Pattern #33

Diagonal
Floral Spray
Pattern #32

Note: all the stems and leaf seams have been overcast in white wool or cotton.

PATTERN #32: "Diagonal Floral Spray I"*

Second Page

diagonal design would be particularly effective pointing inward from the four corners of a quilt. It should be simple enough for those wanting multiple versions of this design to substitute alternate blooms on these stems. Undoubtedly the original of this block was done by separate unit appliqué with discrete stems, leaves, and flowers. It is so easily done by cutwork appliqué that our pattern is drafted for that method. The blooms appear to be padded and the maker has made the block quite elegant by extensive embroidery, probably in wool. In the interests of saving space, the spray of roses (Pattern #32) is shown on the right-hand diagonal half of this four-page pattern, the apple bough (Pattern #33) on the left-hand side.

This embroidery line is drawn on quadrant #1 only. If you'd prefer not to do all those embellishing stitches, the leaves and stems have been drawn for cutaway appliqué.

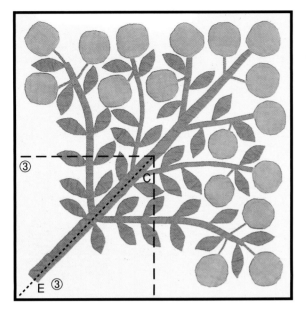

PATTERN #33: "Diagonal Bough of Apples"*
(Shown with Pattern #32)

Third Page

Type: Baltimore-style

To make this block, refer to *Volume I*, Lessons 1 or 2, 5, or 10. See also Appendix I in this book.

Detail: Quilt #1 in the Color Section.

Apples recur in the classic Baltimore Album Quilts. In the most ornate blocks, they nest in baskets or tumble out of cornucopias. In simpler blocks, they come in wreaths, as in quilt #4 (block B-2 and D-4) in the Color Section. This laden apple branch is a much rarer depiction of the fruit. A look at its symbolism shows a significantly different meaning for a bough of apples as opposed to apples in general. A single apple symbolizes Perpetual Concord, and Salvation when depicted in Christ's hands (or

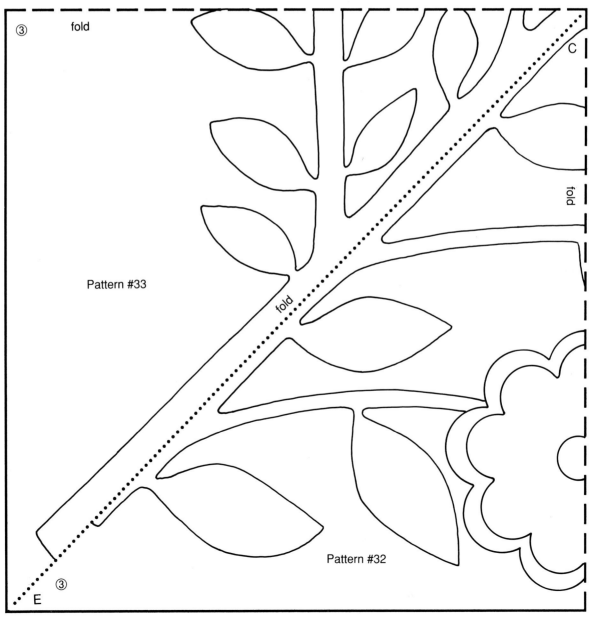

③ fold

C

fold

fold

Pattern #33

Pattern #32

③

E

PATTERN #33: "Diagonal Bough of Apples"*

Fourth Page

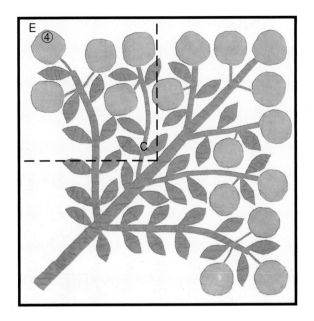

temptation in Adam's hands). But an apple bough harkens back to Greek mythology, signifying Transport to Elysium where, the dictionary reminds us, the Elysian Fields are located. Hence Elysian as an adjective means "happy, blissful, delightful." The Elysian Fields were where virtuous people went after death, a concept which translated in Christianity to Heaven. Elysium is any place or condition of ideal bliss or complete happiness. Hardly disputable intents for an Album quilt!

Going back even further to ancient Hebraic times, Love and Fertility are symbolized by the apple. Barth tells us that Hebrew women who wanted to bear a child mixed the sap of an apple tree with their bathwater, and that Norse gods ate apples to attain perpetual youth. Could that possibly have evolved into the familiar "An apple a day keeps the doctor away"? For my appliqué time, I'd sooner invest in the Elysian field theory!

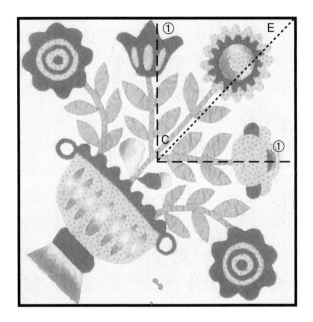

PATTERN #34: "Folk Art Vase of Flowers"*
(Shown with Pattern #35)

Type: Classic "Baltimore"

To make this block, refer to *Volume I*, Lessons 1 or 2, 5, or 10.

Detail: Quilt #3 in the Color Section.

This is a brightly beautiful diagonally set vase of flowers. If you're looking for blocks which can point in towards the center of your quilt, this is one of only a handful of possibilities. Dr. Dunton notes (in *Old Quilts*, p. 27) that "the base of the vase is of the shaded [rainbow fabric] blue, but a very narrow portion at the bottom is tan, indicating that these shaded blues were cut from a striped fabric." This is one of several blocks in quilt #3 that I would describe as "Folk Art"-style. See also Pattern #9.

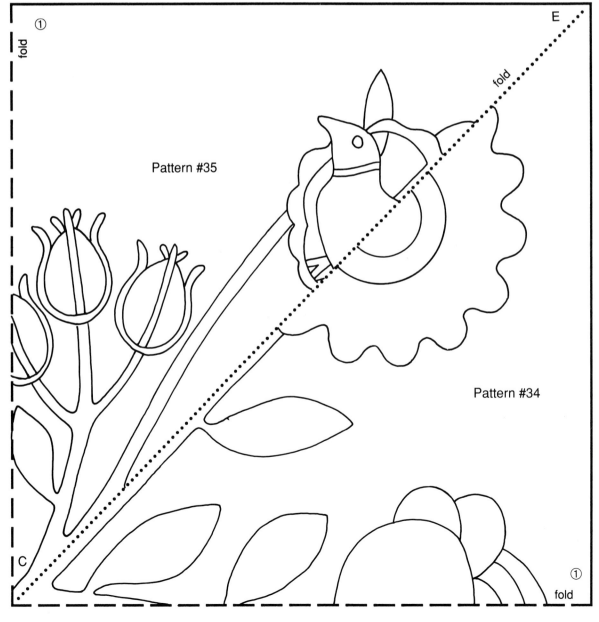

Pattern #35

Pattern #34

PATTERN #34: "Folk Art Vase of Flowers"*

Second Page

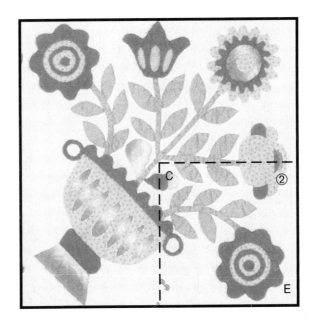

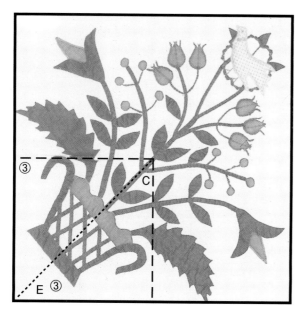

PATTERN #35: "Bird Bedecked Bouquet"*
(Shown with Pattern #34)

Third Page

Type: Baltimore-style

To make this block, refer to *Volume I*, Lessons 1, 5, 9, or 10.

Detail: Quilt #1 in the Color Section.

Charming, and not overly difficult, this block would seem to wish for babies. Filled with buds, a bird on a nest (as yet empty), and cherries (for Sweet Character?), this block seems destined for a Bride's Quilt. The block's maker would seem to be giving her blessing upon what she hopes will be a fruitful union.

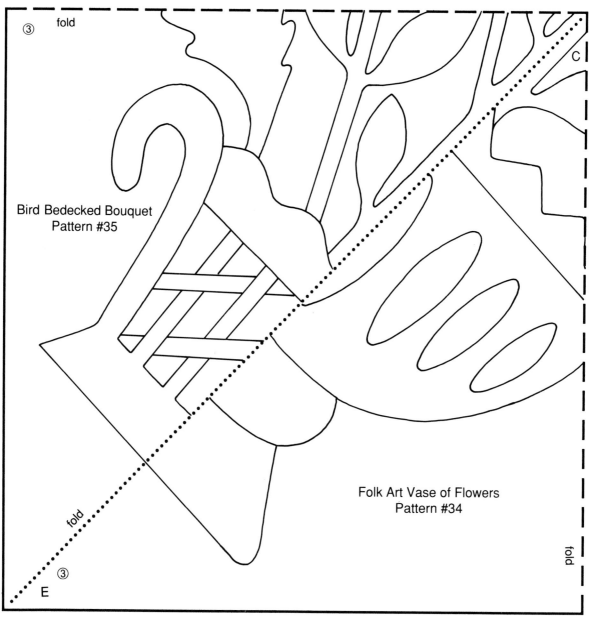

Bird Bedecked Bouquet
Pattern #35

Folk Art Vase of Flowers
Pattern #34

PATTERN #35: "Bird Bedecked Bouquet"*

Fourth Page

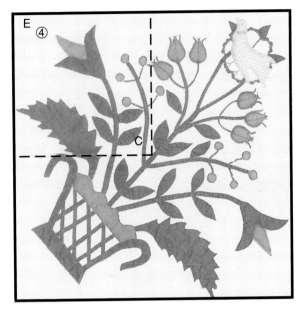

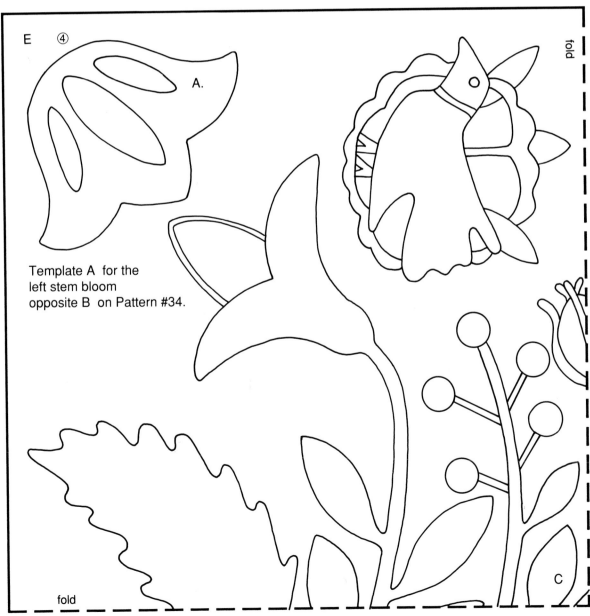

Template A for the
left stem bloom
opposite B on Pattern #34.

fold

PATTERN #36: "Victorian Vase of Flowers III"*

Type: Classic "Baltimore"

To make this block, refer to *Volume I*, Lessons 5, 9, or 10. See also Appendix I in this book.

Detail: Quilt #2 in the Color Section.

Many who dream of Album Quilts, dream of such a block, for this sort of ornate, realistic, Victorian block is one of the characteristic styles of the classic Baltimore Album Quilts. Today's needleartist will observe that the contours of this neoclassic vase have been cleverly depicted by a sophisticated rainbow print which suggests its three-dimensional quality. The print usage progresses upward in a delightful mixture of subtly shaded prints and solids, small calico-like prints, and cut-out motifs to show leaves and flowers. That print of a brown circle forming the center of the blue flowers is one familiar to us in these quilts, as is the convention of splitting fruits

PATTERN #36: "Victorian Vase of Flowers III"*

Second Page

and depicting a bird's eye with a flower. She will have admired (and possibly by now have herself done some of) the inking of moss rose hairs, stems, and leaf veins. Today's quiltmaker will be intrigued by the variety of floral forms and may wonder if this is a particularly original rendition of the three red, one white full-blown rose theme. (See the notes for Pattern #29.)

But what if you were the Victorian quiltmaker who designed this or so many similar blocks of vases and flowers? Might you intend this to be an urn, a footed or pedestaled vase? Long used to hold the ashes of the dead after cremation, the urn can figuratively imply the Grave; flowers, the Soul Heaven Bound; and the bird signifying Life of the Soul, promising immortality in Resurrection. Or, if a dove, symbolizing Innocence, the Holy Spirit, and, again, bearing the message of salvation.

PATTERN #36: "Victorian Vase of Flowers III"*

Third Page

If you lived in mid-nineteenth-century Baltimore, as this block's maker surely must have, your design vocabulary would be permeated by the symbolism of fraternal orders; an urn of flowers would seem the perfect mode for depicting the pot of incense, for indeed it was at times so depicted in Masonic renderings. You would know that the pot of incense is the emblem of a pure heart, "which is always an acceptable sacrifice to the Deity; and, as this glows with fervent heat, so should our hearts continually glow with gratitude to the great beneficent Author of our existence, for the manifold blessings and comforts we enjoy."[13] And, had you been a Daughter of Rebekah, you would know to present this symbol a bit differently, still, perhaps as an urn of flowers, but that pot of incense would be shown sitting upon the altar, even on a simple slab, for burning incense. And why

PATTERN #36: "Victorian Vase of Flowers III"*

Fourth Page

would you not note that this was what you were depicting? Ah, yes, quite right. How silly of me to ask. Everybody does know it.

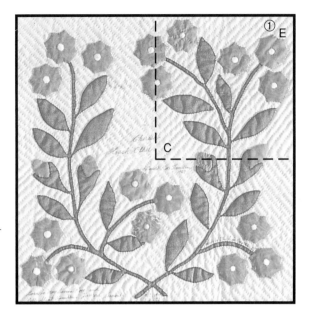

PATTERN #37: "Asymmetrical Spray of Red Blossoms I"*

Type: Classic "Baltimore"

To make this block, refer to *Volume I*, Lessons 1 or 2, and 5.

Detail: *Volume I*, quilt #6.

This arrangement of these unnamed flowers is repeated over and over in the classic Baltimore Album Quilts, with only slight variations. Gracefully balanced in asymmetry, an aesthetic quality much sought after by the makers of these classic quilts, one can understand why the block was so well-loved. And speaking of love, if I had to guess, I'd say, both from the flower and the frequency with which it is portrayed, that we are looking at a rosebush.

I approached this block by doing the green as one piece by cutwork appliqué. The flowers I did by needle-turn, and reverse appliquéd or buttonholed most of the centers. A few centers I did over a plastic template cut by

PATTERN #37: "Asymmetrical Spray of Red Blossoms I"*

Second Page

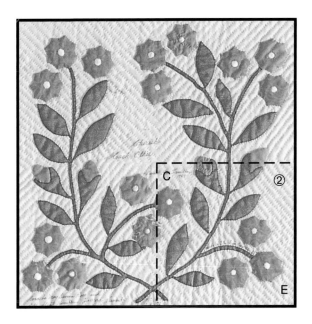

a paper punch using the methods described in Lesson 9 (*Volume I*). Possibly you can recognize these for their more precise circular shape.

I can't resist concluding this botannical conjecture with a quote reported in *The Heyday of Natural History* (p. 114) which cuts periously close to needlewomen, including the quiltmakers of today as well as of yesterday. In addition, it reminds us of the quantity of publications available on botanical themes in the 1840s and 1850s. "Charles Kingsley reported patronizingly at the height of the [fern collecting] craze that it was having an entirely beneficial effect on the nation's womenfolk: Your daughters, perhaps, have been seized with the prevailing 'Pteridomania,' wrangling over unpronounceable names of species (which seem to be different in each new fern book they buy) till Pteridomania seems to you somewhat

PATTERN #37: "Asymmetrical Spray of Red Blossoms I"*

Third Page

of a bore: and yet you cannot deny that they find an enjoyment in it, and are more active, more cheerful, more self-forgetful over it, than they would have been over novels and gossips, crochet and Berlin-wool. At least you will confess that the abomination of 'Fancy work,' that standing cloak for dreamy idleness, has all but vanished from your drawing-room since the 'Lady-ferns' and 'Venus's hair' appeared."

PATTERN #37: "Asymmetrical Spray of Red Blossoms I"*

Fourth Page

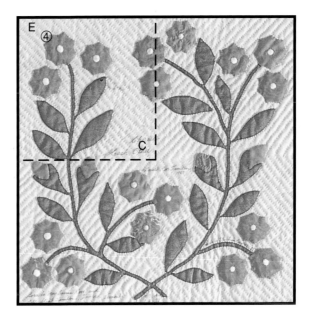

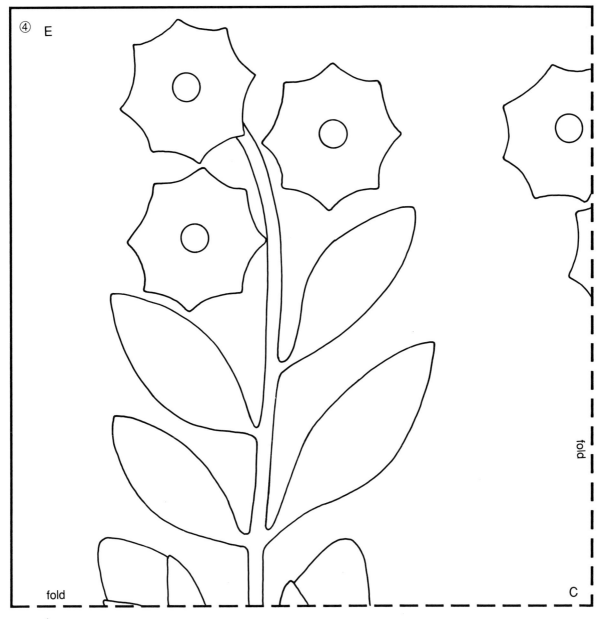

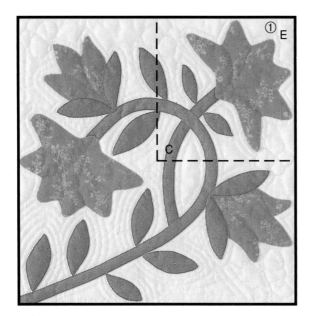

PATTERN #38: "Peony Medallion Center"*

Type: Possibly "Beyond"

To make this block, refer to *Volume I*, Lessons 5, 9, and 10. See also Appendix I in this book.

Detail: *Volume I*, quilt #7.

One of the significant aspects of the classic quilts, discussed in *Volume II*, is the various sets of the Baltimore Album Quilts. While the twenty-five-block set (5 x 5) seems the most typical (and has a clear center), there are many quilts in a sixteen-block set which, being even numbered, do not have a center block. Many of the classic quilts' makers seem to have tried to organize the Album's blocks and to create an internal design, often with a focus on the center. Thus the focus in quilt #2 in the Color Section is on the central four building blocks which have the effect of a central medallion.

PATTERN #38: "Peony Medallion Center"*

Second Page

I have called this pattern's flower the "peony," for so it appears to me. Moreover, peonies have the pleasing symbolism of Healing. In the original quilt,[14] the same repeat block center medallion is in a thirty-six-block quilt. It forms the center of quilt #8 (*Volume I*) with thirty-six blocks, and of quilt #7, with sixteen blocks. One other quilt, a classic Baltimore Album,[15] displays this same style of a four-repeat block center. But in that quilt, it is sixteen large strawberries that form the quilt's medallion center focus. To get this peony block pattern to face both left and right, trace the pattern onto a 12½"-square sheet of paper, then trace the reverse of it on a lightbox. The two patterns form the four blocks used for the central medallion.

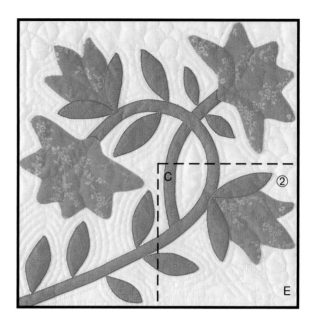

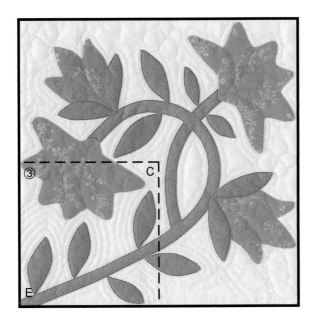

PATTERN #38: "Peony Medallion Center"*

Third Page

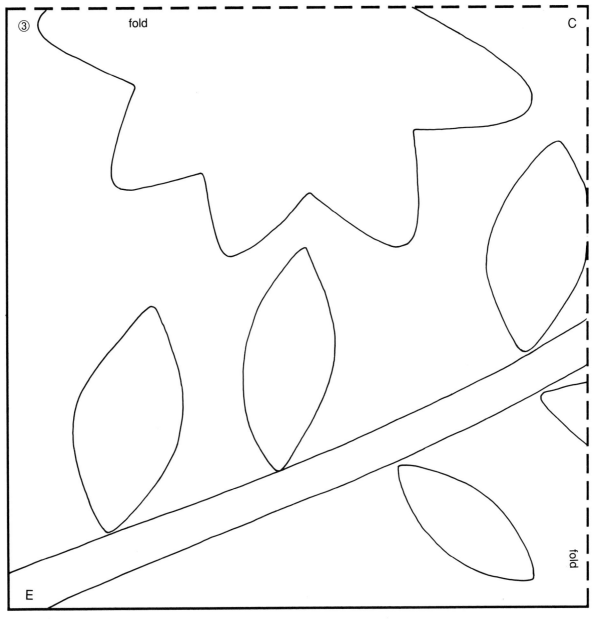

PATTERN #38: "Peony Medallion Center"*

Fourth Page

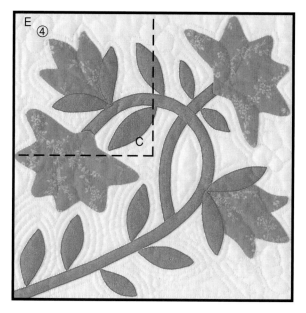

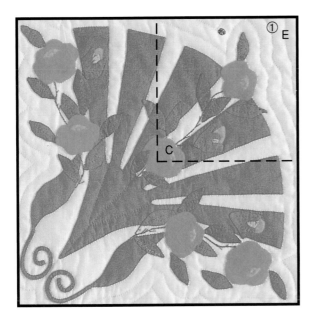

PATTERN #39: "Albertine's Rose Climber"*

Type: "Beyond"

To make this block, refer to *Volume I*, Lessons 1 or 2, 5, and 10. See also Appendix I in this book.

Detail: *Volume I*, quilt #7.

This block is an original design by Albertine Veenstra. Appearing in two slightly varied versions in quilt #7 (*Volume I*), it's one of the blocks for which people seem most to want a pattern. This version is based on Albertine's design. Her roses are done in a glossy sateen and are embellished with skillfully embroidered stem, outline, or crewel stitch (they are essentially all the same stitch). This pattern shows a layered rose, another design possibility.

PATTERN #39: "Albertine's Rose Climber"*

Second Page

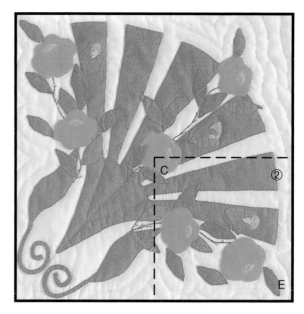

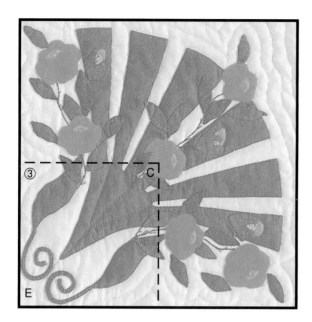

PATTERN #39: "Albertine's Rose Climber"*

Third Page

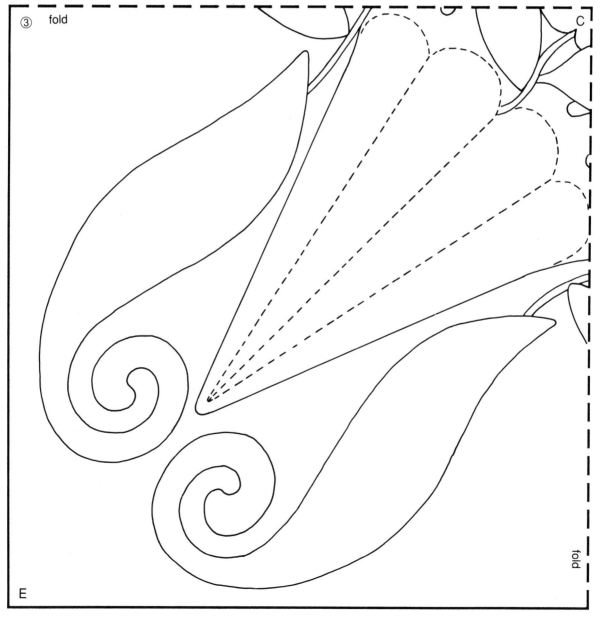

PATTERN #39: "Albertine's Rose Climber"*

Fourth Page

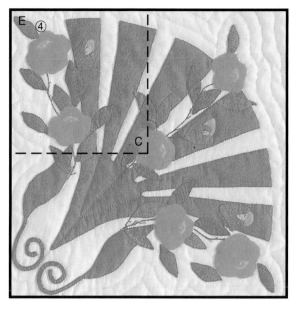

PATTERN #40: "Victorian Basket of Flowers II"*

Type: Classic "Baltimore"

To make this block, refer to *Volume I*, Lessons 5, 9, or 10. See also Appendix I in this book.

Detail: *Volume I*, quilt #2.

A charming basket, this is the fullest and therefore the most complex in this book. For one's first basket, Pattern #41 is a better choice.

PATTERN #40: "Victorian Basket of Flowers II"*

Second Page

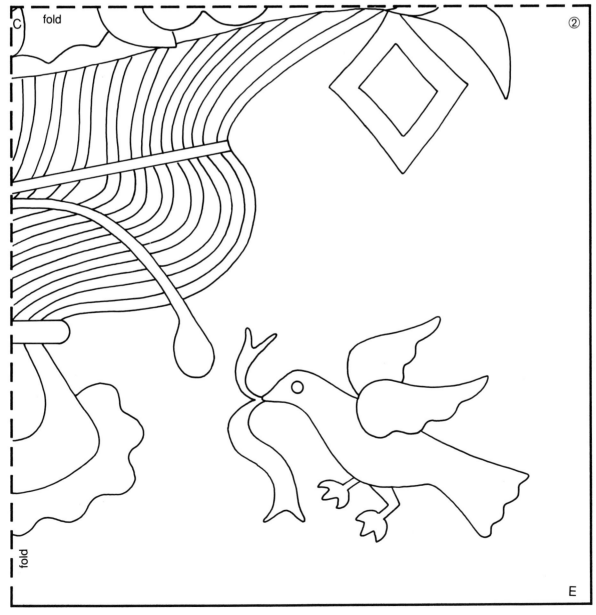

PATTERN #40: "Victorian Basket of Flowers II"*

Third Page

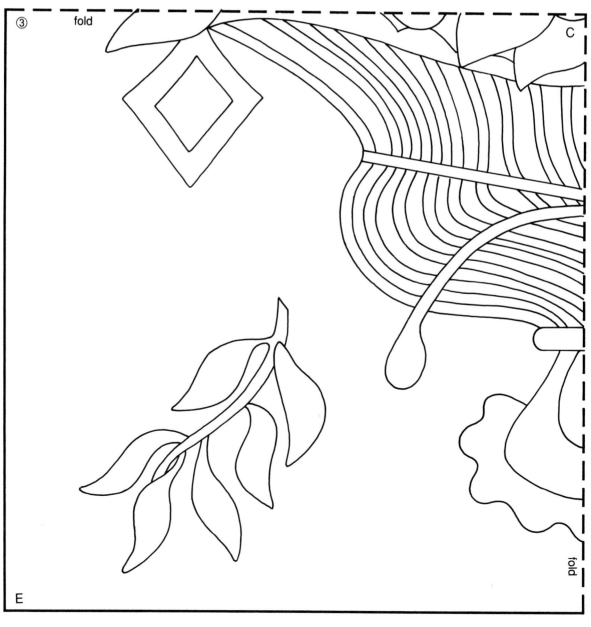

PATTERN #40: "Victorian Basket of Flowers II"*

Fourth Page

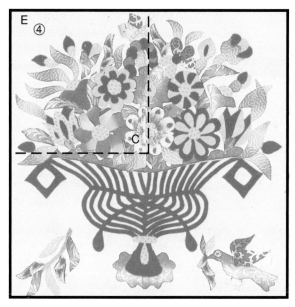

PATTERN #41: "Victorian Basket of Flowers IV"*

Type: Classic "Baltimore"

To make this block, refer to *Volume I*, Lessons 5, 9, or 10. See also Appendix I in this book.

Detail: *Volume I*, quilt #2.

Ornate, realistic, Victorian, a woven basket—and yet not overwhelming at that. This basket, with a bit of ruffled trim at the bottom, is a style repeated in an exquisite Album Quilt belonging to the Smithsonian Institution in Washington.

The second, third, and fourth pages of Pattern #41 follow the Color Section.

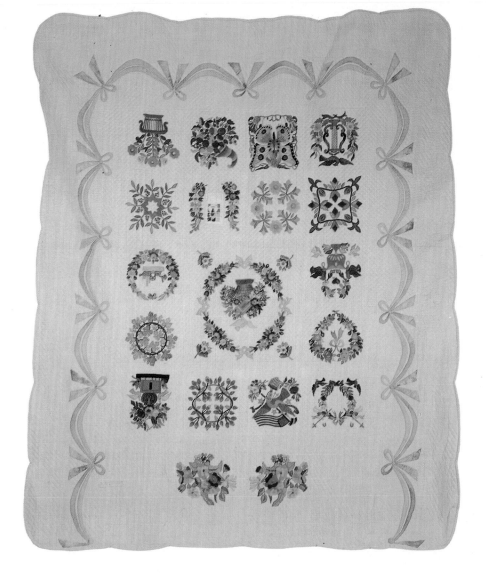

QUILT #6.
CONTEMPORARY BALTIMORE-STYLE
ALBUM QUILT

Esther Rose Jackson interpreted the classic Baltimore block patterns from *Spoken Without a Word* perfectly to her taste to create this elegant quilt. Its set and color scheme, tailored for a particular bed and decor, place the quilt distinctively "Beyond" Baltimore. Esther's Baltimore Album is quilted in ⅝" diagonals with "tear drop," double-feathered wreath and freehand-drawn patterns. Approximately 90" x 108". 1985–88. (Photo: E. Jackson)

While sets and borders are primarily the subject of *Volume II*, these two 1980s Album Quilts differ so in set from any classic Baltimore Quilts that they are included here for further inspiration.

QUILT #5. CONTEMPORARY APPLIQUÉD ALBUM QUILT

Sometimes a quilt is exceptional because it reflects the maker's personal aesthetic clearly and uniquely. While not closely tied to the Baltimore style either by color or by block patterns, Ruby Ollivier's quilt is a dramatically successful contemporary appliquéd Album Quilt. Ruby used commercial patterns ("center block, *Ladies' Circle Patchwork Quilts*, July 1988; border, Shirley Thompson's *It's Not a Quilt Until It's Quilted*, plus others") and melded them with a love for sculptural shapes and colonial colors. 72" x 72". 1988–89. (Photo: The Jadwinds Studio)

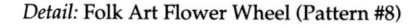

Detail: Folk Art Flower Wheel (Pattern #8)

QUILT #4. CLASSIC BALTIMORE ALBUM QUILT

This exuberantly elegant quilt is inscribed in part "Ladies of Baltimore" and "1848." An ornate running rose vine border frames a wealth of classic Album block styles in this tour de force. Both the complex cutwork rose border design and the illusion of a Greek cross in the center of the traditional twenty-five block set are echoed in other classic Baltimore Albums. Accession #1:1973. Gift of Mrs. Stratford Lee Morton. (Photo: St. Louis Art Museum)

Detail: Wreath of Roses, (Pattern #20)

QUILT #3. CLASSIC BALTIMORE ALBUM QUILT

A meandering vine border with padded roses and buds encloses the whole which is set in a carefully wrought balance. This is a beautiful quilt, from its brightly varied block styles, to the intricacy of its embroidery and inking. It was extensively recorded by Dr. William Rush Dunton in *Old Quilts*. The focus of the quilt seems to be on both the center block (a monument like that inscribed "Ringgold," Baltimore's fallen Mexican War hero, in Shelburne's Baltimore-style Album) and on the Rose Wreath above it, inscribed "To the Gray Boys." A Christian ("Latin") cross seems formed in the center by these blocks' set. Also inscribed on the quilt is "Mrs. John Mann, Eutaw Street, Baltie." (Photo: © 1988 Sotheby's, Inc., New York)

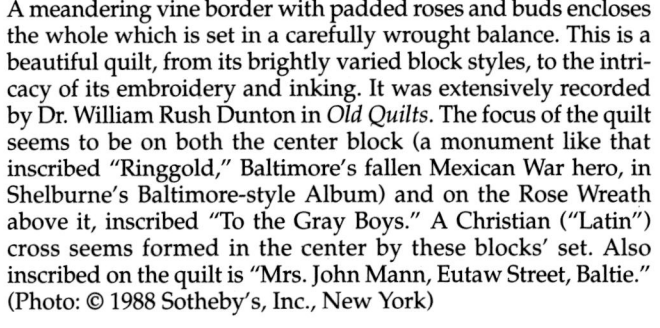

QUILT #2. CLASSIC BALTIMORE-STYLE ALBUM QUILT

Surely one of the most exquisite of the Baltimore Album Quilts,
this circa 1850 masterpiece is mysteriously undocumented. No
inscriptions have been found upon it, yet it seems unmistakably
identifiable by style, themes, fabrics, and buildings as Classic
Baltimore. A large-scale, lush botanical print was used extensively
in the border and in several of the blocks. This, the four-building
center to the sixteen-block set, and the differing border corners
all add to the quilt's unique look within the genre. The heavily
stuffed and possibly tea-dyed border centers on a beehive nestled
in flowers and swarming with inked bees. Accession #76.609.6.
Gift of Mr. and Mrs. Foster McCarl, Jr. 92" x 91½". (Photo: Abby
Aldrich Rockefeller Folk Art Center, Williamsburg, Virginia)

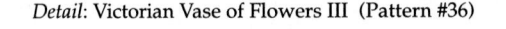

Detail: Victorian Vase of Flowers III (Pattern #36)

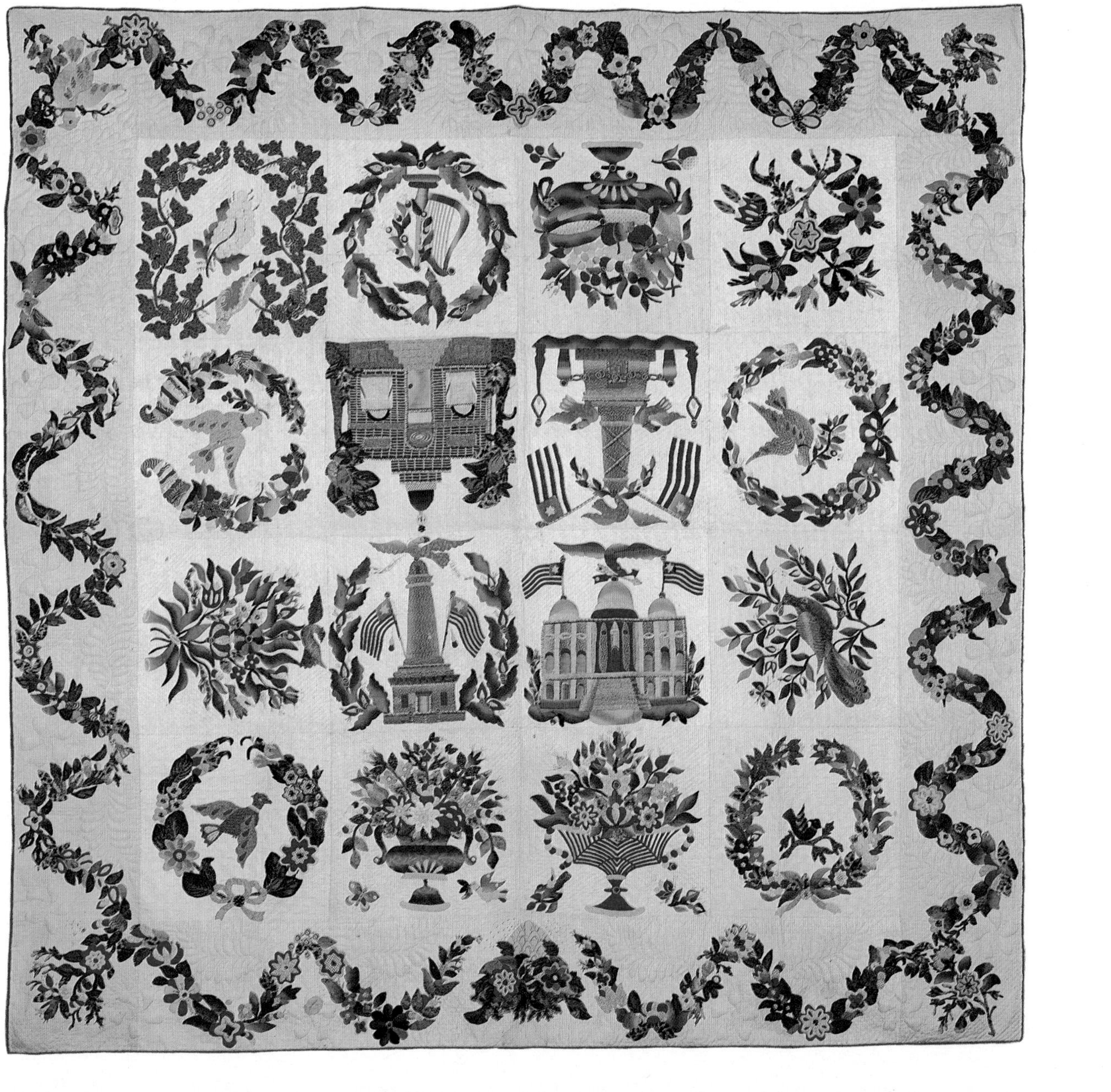

39

40

39. PEACOCK PASTORALE (Pattern #54).
    (Photo: © 1987 Sotheby's, Inc., New York)

40. *BOUQUET AVEC TROIS OISEAUX* (Pattern #47). Detail: Baltimore Album Quilt. Accession #76.609.6. Gift of Mr. and Mrs. Foster McCarl, Jr. (Photo: Abby Aldrich Rockefeller Folk Art Center, Williamsburg, Virginia)

41. LYRE WITH WREATH, BIRD, AND CROWN (Pattern #48). Detail: Baltimore Album Quilt. Accession #76.609.6. Gift of Mr. and Mrs. Foster McCarl, Jr. (Photo: Abby Aldrich Rockefeller Folk Art Center, Williamsburg, Virginia)

42. WREATH AND DOVE II (Pattern #55). Detail: Baltimore Album Quilt. Accession #76.609.6. Gift of Mr. and Mrs. Foster McCarl, Jr. (Photo: Abby Aldrich Rockefeller Folk Art Center, Williamsburg, Virginia)

41

35

36

34. VICTORIAN BASKET OF FLOWERS IV (Pattern #41).
(Photo: © 1987 Sotheby's, Inc., New York)

35. LYRE *SCHERENSCHNITTE* (Pattern #3).
Maxine Davis Satchell, 1989.
(Photo: S. Risedorph)

36. FLEUR-DE-LIS WITH ROSEBUDS IV (Pattern #14). Gene Way, 1989.
(Photo: S. Risedorph)

37. FLEUR-DE-LIS II (Pattern #2). Elly Sienkiewicz, 1987.
(Photo: S. Risedorph)

38. ASYMMETRICAL SPRAY OF RED BLOSSOMS I (Pattern #37).
Elly Sienkiewicz, 1985.
(Photo: © G. E. Garrison 1988)

38

34

37

29

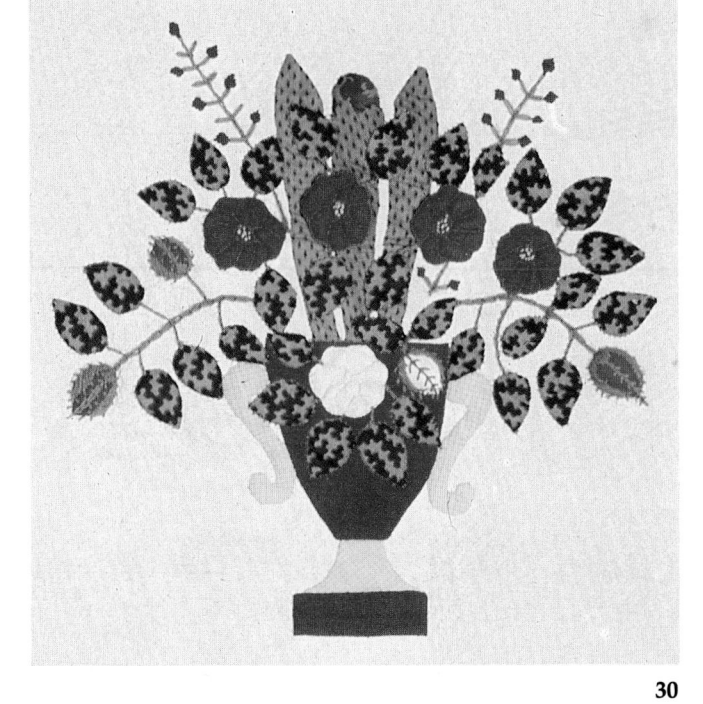

30

29. ALBERTINE'S ROSE CLIMBER (Pattern #39).
Albertine Veenstra, 1984.
(Photo: S. Risedorph)

30. VICTORIAN VASE OF FLOWERS I (Pattern #43).
(Photo: © 1987 Sotheby's, Inc., New York)

31. BETTY ALDERMAN'S *SCHERENSCHNITTE* (Pattern #4).
Donna Scranton, 1989.
(Photo: S. Risedorph)

32. PEONY MEDALLION CENTER (Pattern #38). Kathy Pease, 1986.
(Photo: S. Risedorph)

33. FOUR-RIBBON WREATH (Pattern #56).
(Photo: © 1987 Sotheby's, Inc., New York)

33

31

32

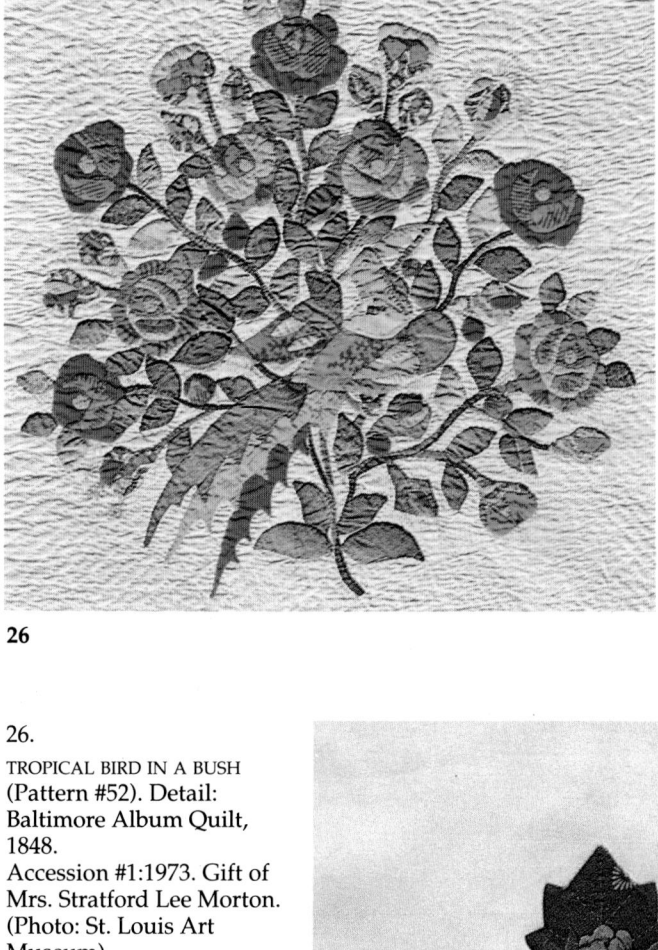

26

27

26.

TROPICAL BIRD IN A BUSH
(Pattern #52). Detail:
Baltimore Album Quilt,
1848.
Accession #1:1973. Gift of
Mrs. Stratford Lee Morton.
(Photo: St. Louis Art
Museum)

27.

CLIPPER SHIP (Pattern #53).
Sylvia Pickell, 1989.
(Photo: S. Risedorph)

28.

GRAPEVINE LYRE WREATH
(Pattern #28).
Elly Sienkiewicz, 1989.
(Photo: S. Risedorph)

28

23

24

23.
MARYLAND MANOR HOUSE
(Pattern #50).
(Photo: © 1987 Sotheby's,
Inc., New York)

24.
SYMBOLIC FOUNTAIN
(Pattern #51).
(Photo: © 1987 Sotheby's,
Inc., New York)

25.
ROSES FOR HANS CHRISTIAN
ANDERSEN (Pattern #27).
Elly Sienkiewicz, 1989.
(Photo: S. Risedorph)

25

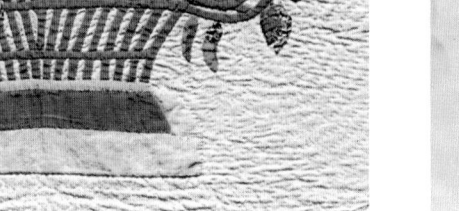

20

21

20.

VICTORIAN BASKET V WITH
FRUITS AND FLOWERS
(Pattern #42). Detail:
Baltimore Album Quilt,
1848. Accession #1:1973.
Gift of Mrs. Stratford Lee
Morton.
(Photo: St. Louis Art
Museum)

21.

CHERRY WREATH WITH
BLUEBIRDS I (Pattern #31).
Elly Sienkiewicz, 1988–89.
(Photo: S. Risedorph)

22.

CORNUCOPIA II (Pattern
#49). (Photo: © 1987
Sotheby's, Inc., New York)

22

17

18

17.
THE ALBUM (Pattern #46).
(Photo: © 1987 Sotheby's,
Inc., New York)

18.
VICTORIAN BASKET OF
FLOWERS II (Pattern #40).
(Photo ©1987 Sotheby's,
Inc., New York)

19.
FLEUR-DE-LIS WITH
ROSEBUDS III (Pattern #13).
Elly Sienkiewicz, 1989.
(Photo: S. Risedorph)

19

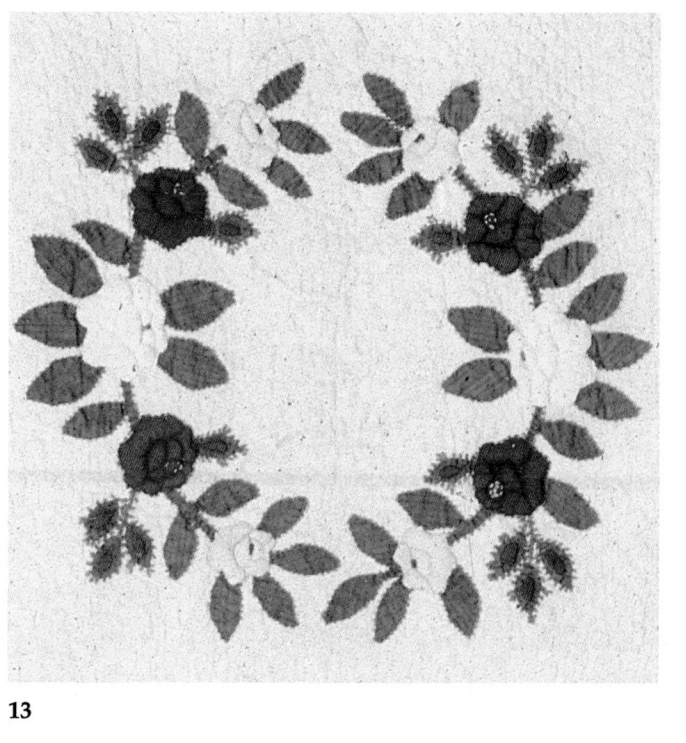

13

13. BROKEN WREATH OF ROSES (Pattern #19).
    (Photo: © 1988 Sotheby's, Inc., New York)

14. CHERRY WREATH WITH BLUEBIRDS II (Pattern #31).
    Lucy Rogers Matteo, 1989.
    (Photo: S. Risedorph)

15. CROSSED SPRAYS OF FLOWERS (Pattern #26).
    (Photo: © 1988 Sotheby's, Inc., New York)

16. FLEUR-DE-LIS MEDALLION II (Pattern #21). Georgia Cibul, 1988.
    (Photo: S. Risedorph)

15

16

9

10

9. SCALLOPED EPERGNE OF FRUIT (Pattern #44).
   (Photo: © 1988 Sotheby's, Inc., New York)

10. MELODIES OF LOVE (Pattern #45).
    (Photo: © 1987 Sotheby's, Inc., New York)

11. FOLK ART VASE OF FLOWERS (Pattern #34).
    (Photo: © 1988 Sotheby's, Inc., New York)

12. FLEUR-DE-LIS MEDALLION I (Pattern #1). Gerri Rathbun, 1990.
    (Photo: S. Risedorph)

12

11

5

6

5. CHRISTMAS CACTUS I (Pattern #12). Nonna Crook, 1985.
   (Photo: © G. E. Garrison 1988)

6. HEARTS AND SWANS II (Pattern #6). Mary Wise Miller, 1989.
   (Photo: S. Risedorph)

7. LYRE WITH LAUREL SPRAYS I (Pattern #25). Detail: Baltimore
   Album Quilt inscribed "Baltimore" and "1846" and
   "1847." Collection of Lee Porter, *Volume I*, quilt #4.
   (Photo: E. Sienkiewicz)

8. ROSE OF SHARON III (Pattern #17). Elly Sienkiewicz, 1984–85.
   (Photo: S. Risedorph)

7

8

1

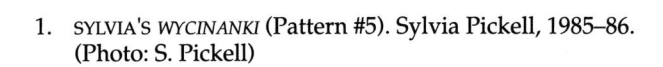

2

1. SYLVIA'S *WYCINANKI* (Pattern #5). Sylvia Pickell, 1985–86.
   (Photo: S. Pickell)

2. HEARTS AND TULIPS (Pattern #9). Elly Sienkiewicz, 1984–85.
   (Photo: © G. E. Garrison 1988)

3. RED VASES AND RED FLOWERS (Pattern #10). Elly Sienkiewicz,
   1984–85.
   (Photo: © G. E. Garrison 1988)

4. VICTORIAN FAVORITE (Pattern #11). Elly Sienkiewicz,
   1984–85. (Photo: © G. E. Garrison 1988)

3

4

The Color Section

THE PATTERN BLOCKS AND THE GALLERY QUILTS

QUILT #1. BALTIMORE-STYLE ALBUM QUILT, circa 1845–50.

Bright, beautiful, and, as Albums go, refreshingly simple, this
appliquéd cotton quilt has some stuffed appliqué with cotton and
wool embroidered embellishments. 89¾" x 90⅜". Gift of Mrs.
Chauncey B. Borland. Accession #1957.524. (Photo: Art Institute
of Chicago)

Patterns for the following blocks from Quilt #1 appear in "Part Two:
The Patterns":
Block C-1: Vase with Fruits and Flowers (Pattern #30); Block B-3:
Rose of Sharon II (Pattern #7); Block B-4: Diagonal Bough of Apples
(Pattern #33); Block B-5: Rose Lyre II (Pattern #22); Block C-2: Rose
Cornucopias (Pattern #24); Block C-4: Strawberry Wreath II (Pattern
#16); Block C-5: Bird Bedecked Bouquet (Pattern #35); Block D-1:
Grapevine Wreath II (Pattern #15); Block D-2: Circular Sprays of
Flowers (Pattern #18); Block D-3: Diagonal Floral Spray I (Pattern
#32); Block D-5: Redbird Lyre (Pattern #23).

Detail: Vase of Full-Blown Roses IV (Pattern #29)

PATTERN #41: "Victorian Basket of Flowers IV"*

Second Page

PATTERN #41: "Victorian Basket of Flowers IV"*

Third Page

PATTERN #41: "Victorian Basket of Flowers IV"*

Fourth Page

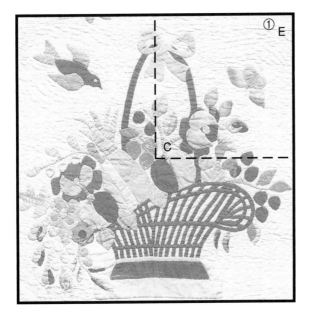

PATTERN #42: "Victorian Basket V with Fruits and Flowers"*

Type: Classic "Baltimore"

To make this block, refer to *Volume I*, Lesson 5, 7, 9, or 10. See also Appendix I in this book.

Detail: Quilt #4 in the Color Section.

This particularly graceful basket shape is usually filled with flowers. In an artful play on that theme, this one includes fruit as well. The elegant touch of what may be a pearl-handled fruit knife usually accompanies a cut watermelon. Here it is seen with a fresh pineapple, symbol of Hospitality and imbued with the message "You are perfect!" Bird, butterfly, basket, and contents are probably replete with symbolic intent, but that is left for you to decipher!

PATTERN #42: "Victorian Basket V with Fruits and Flowers"*

Second Page

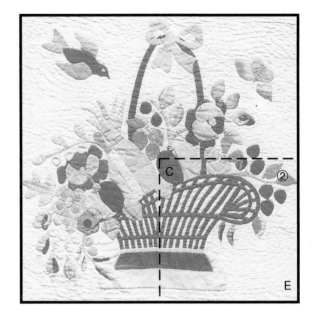

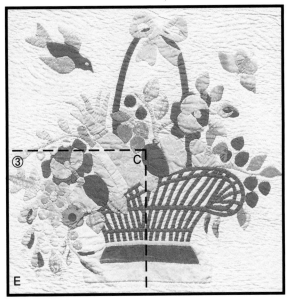

PATTERN #42: "Victorian Basket V with Fruits and Flowers"*

Third Page

PATTERN #42: "Victorian Basket V with Fruits and Flowers"*

Fourth Page

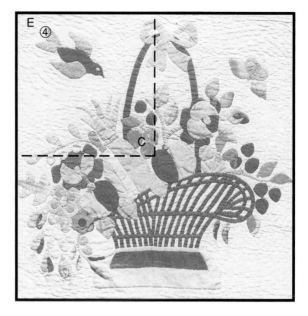

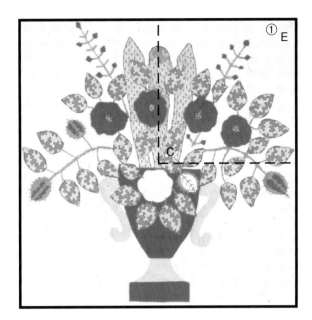

PATTERN #43: "Victorian Vase of Flowers I"*

Type: Classic "Baltimore"

To make this block, refer to *Volume I*, Lessons 5, 9, or 10. See also Appendix I in this book.

Detail: Quilt #4 in the Color Section.

A most endearing neoclassical vase of flowers, this appears to be one of a kind. It is a bit smaller than the other blocks in its quilt and it is so depicted here. The appliqué is quite straightforward, and moderately time-consuming. But the embroidery, which really makes this block visually, will also make it take considerably longer to do.

PATTERN #43: "Victorian Vase of Flowers I"*

Second Page

PATTERN #43: "Victorian Vase of Flowers I"*

Third Page

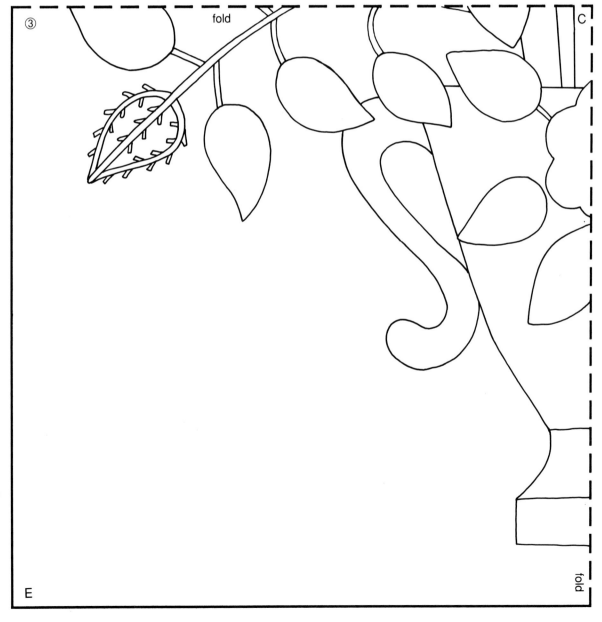

PATTERN #43: "Victorian Vase of Flowers I"*

Fourth Page

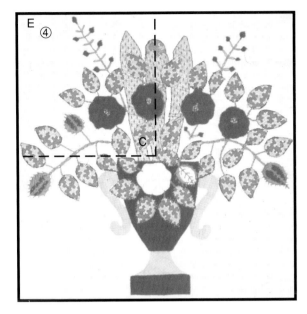

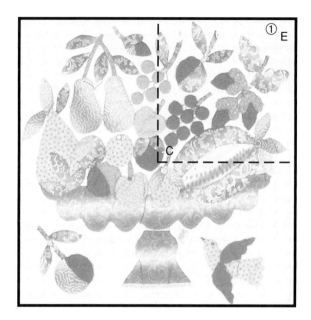

PATTERN #44: "Scalloped Epergne of Fruit"*

Type: Classic "Baltimore"

To make this block, refer to *Volume I*, Lesson 5, 9, or 10. See also Appendix I in this book.

Detail: Quilt #3 in the Color Section.

Our block presents a highly stylized version of the fruit in a raised glass stand motif. Epergnes—pedestaled, ornamental serving dishes—were a popular decorative glassware at the time of this quilt's making. In elegant variety, epergnes were depicted in some detail in these Album Quilts. My observation, by no means definitive, is that this scalloped version comes early on the chart of these quilts as in this 1846–47 quilt. By contrast, some, possibly later, epergnes are depicted in finer detail, often with cut glass ornamentation on the bowl.

Some rather sophisticated fabric adds to the elegance of this block. Dr. Dunton describes it in his usual exact

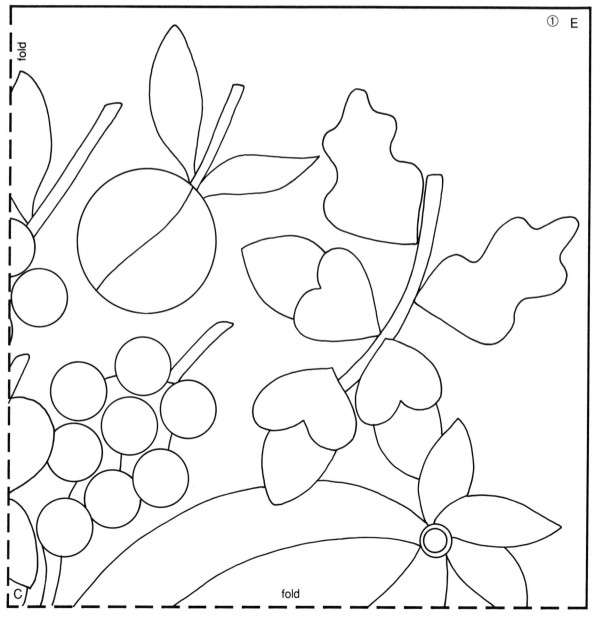

PATTERN #44: "Scalloped Epergne of Fruit"*

Second Page

manner: "The watermelon is of a shaded and figured green with meat of a figured pink stripe and inked seeds. Two other figured prints form the fruit. The pineapple is the...yellow [print with very small black dots and larger dots encircled with small dots] with the same figured green as the watermelon. This is also used for the foliage of the upper fruits and of the fruit in the lower left corner, the right half being red. The upper bunch of grapes is blue, the lower red. The three strawberries to the right are red, their seeds indicated with white stitching. Their hulls are a figured green.... The pears on the upper left are of a moire green shaded to white" (*Old Quilts*, p. 22).

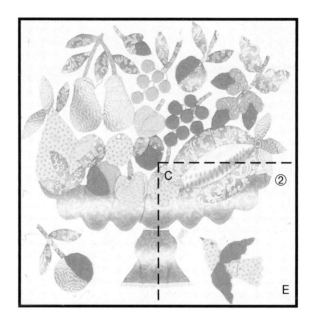

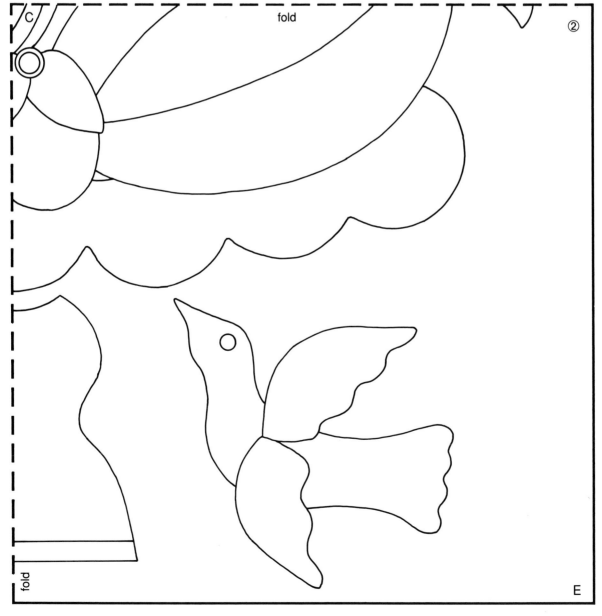

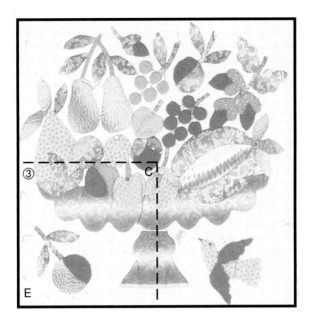

PATTERN #44: "Scalloped Epergne of Fruit"*

Third Page

PATTERN #44: "Scalloped Epergne of Fruit"*

Fourth Page

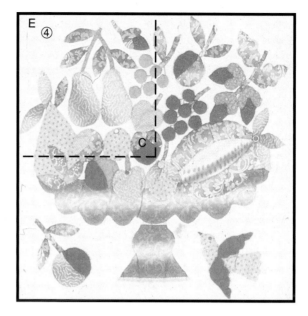

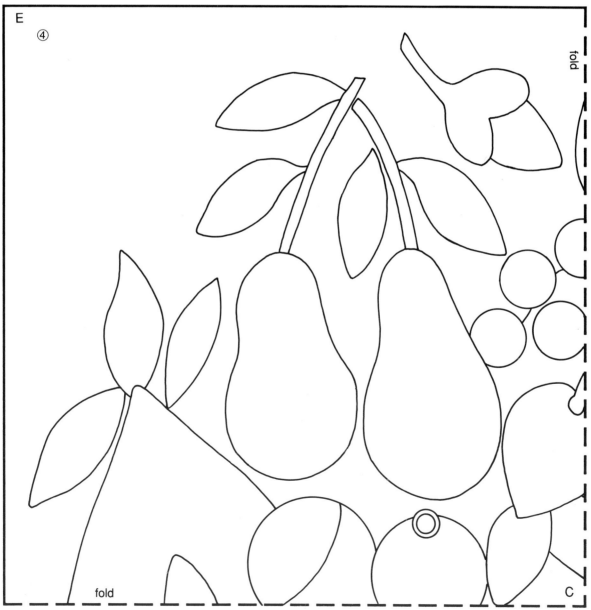

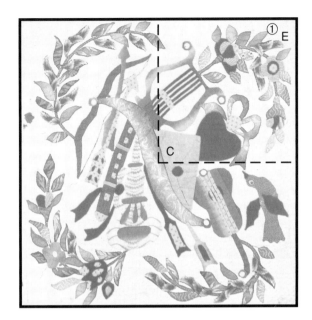

PATTERN #45: "Melodies of Love"*

Type: Classic "Baltimore"

To make this block, refer to *Volume I*, Lesson(s) 5, 9, or 10. See also Appendix I in this book.

Detail: *Volume I*, quilt #2.

Love and music—oh, sweet harmony!—would seem to be the theme here. The block appears to have both romantic and neoclassical overtones, with a heart, sealed epistle, music, and arrows symbolizing Romantic Love through the god Eros amid fronds of graceful flowers. Despite the visual appeal of this pattern, I've only seen two other blocks,[16] all three slightly different, which depict it. This sort of decorative motif might be expected to be familiar to the Baltimore Albums' makers from printed textiles in vogue at the time. That decorative arts source might in itself explain this complex and not often repeated design.

PATTERN #45: "Melodies of Love"*

Second Page

This music block might be a reference to one or more of the German social clubs, many of which emphasized musical themes as a basis for fraternizing. Close to 200,000 German immigrants entered through the Port of Baltimore in the three decades before the Civil War. Some took off to settle the Midwest but a sizeable number stayed in Baltimore. The Germans who had come earlier had farmed the frontier and turned Baltimore into a major grain port. By midcentury, they had been virtually assimilated.

Many of the newer German immigrants prospered in the tobacco export trade, but with a few notable exceptions they were regarded as foreigners. They faced a formidable language barrier and, on top of this, they seemed to prefer their own kind and their own customs. What developed was a social system consisting of an "elaborate organization of clubs, each catering to a

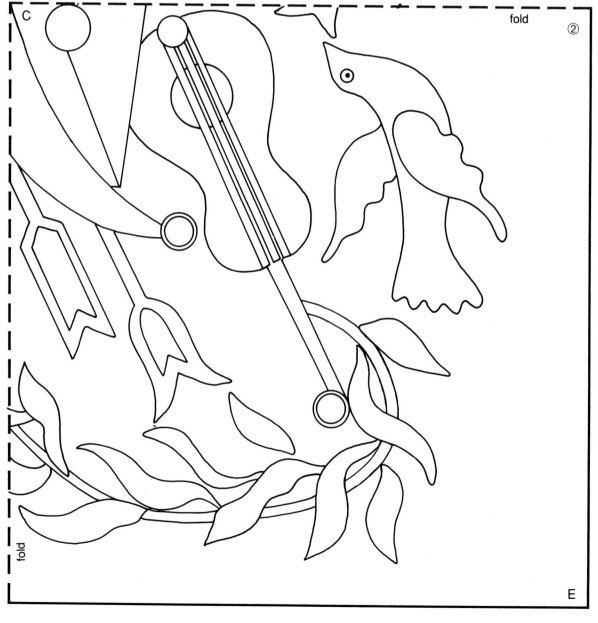

PATTERN #45: "Melodies of Love"*

Third Page

different class. At the top of the pile was the Germania Club which was founded in 1840. It was the most exclusive of all and its membership was confined to the wealthy merchants.... Next to the Germania in social importance was the Concordia, founded in 1847. This club emphasized a literary and musical program that appealed to the intellectuals of the upper middle class. Its musical and dramatic divisions sponsored ambitious productions that gave it unusual distinctions. A cut below the Germania and the Concordia were the singing societies. The oldest of these was the Liederkranz which was organized in 1836 out of the choir of Zion Church.... Other singing societies stemming from choirs and catering to a lower social group were the Harmonie and the Arion. On the other hand, the German Mannechor, founded in 1856, was reserved primarily for the families of the wealthy merchants. These various singing societies

PATTERN #45: "Melodies of Love"*

Fourth Page

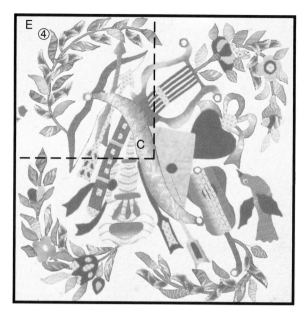

met annually with similar societies in Philadelphia and other cities for a national sangerfest. At the bottom of the social scale were the gymnastic clubs. These appealed to the rank and file of immigrants and were part of the Turner movement whose basic concept was a healthy mind in a healthy body."[17]

There is also a musical instrument of some sort in the central block (*Volume I*, quilt #2 in the Color Section) in which this pattern I've dubbed "Melodies of Love" appears. The musical instrument, seemingly symbolic, appears with our national emblem, the eagle (Courage, Generosity, Highest Inspiration, Resurrection) in whose talons the bundle of arrows signifies Unity. The other leg's talons clasp a branch of laurel (Triumph, Victory, Eternity) and the Phrygian cap, symbol of freedom from slavery. On his breast the eagle wears a shield, signifying

continued on page 173

PATTERN #46: "The Album"*

Type: Classic "Baltimore"

To make this block, refer to *Volume I*, Lesson 7, 5, 9, and 10. See also Appendix I in this book.

Detail: *Volume I*, quilt #2.

"The Album" seems increasingly to inform our sense of these quilts, for as all albums are collections upon a theme, so, too, are Album Quilts. The themes of these Album Quilts seem to vary widely and many remain elusive. A favorite Album block in the ornate, realistic, Victorian style, is the bird holding a book above flowers: flowers in a basket, or, as here, in a wreath. The books are commonly labeled, for which we are grateful! Some are marked Bible, others Sacred Melodies, some Album, some have a person's name inscribed on them, and most seem to have a ribbon in them marking a

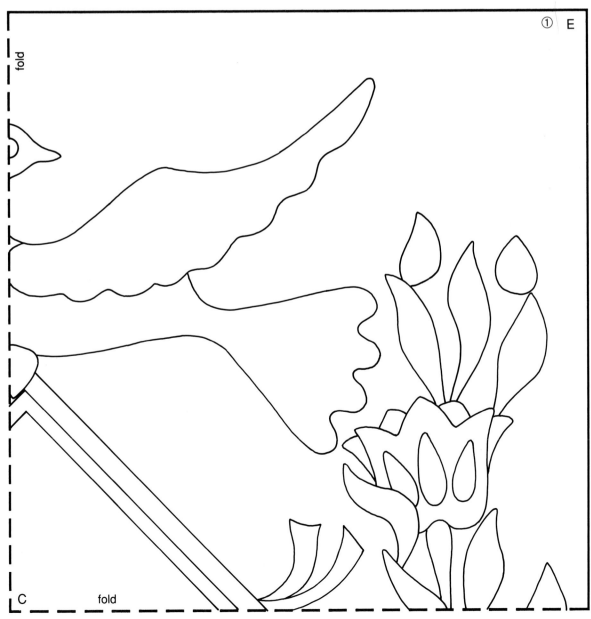

PATTERN #46: "The Album"*

Second Page

page. This elegant block is complex, yet approachable, and would make a wonderful addition to any of our Albums!

PATTERN #46: "The Album"*

Third Page

PATTERN #46: "The Album"*

Fourth Page

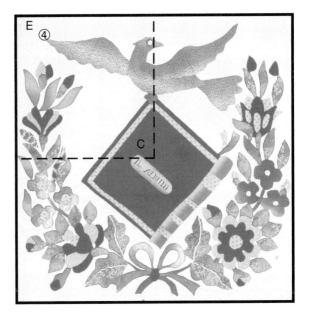

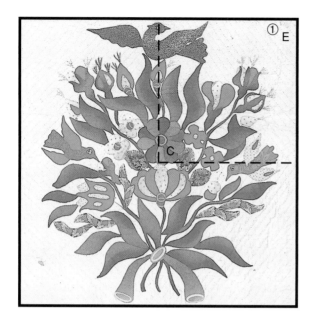

PATTERN #47: *"Bouquet avec Trois Oiseaux"**

Type: Classic "Baltimore"

To make this block, refer to *Volume I*, Lessons 5, 7, 9, or 10. See also Appendix I in this book.

Detail: Quilt #2 in the Color Section.

An exquisite block, but why the French? To help gain understanding of these quilts, I have been studying autograph and other albums of the 1840s through the 1870s. One, an 1870s autograph album in the manuscript collection of the Winterthur Museum, is replete with calligraphy, poems, sketches, inscriptions from as far apart as New York and Atlanta, and some French! One person addresses the album's owner, *Ma chère Camille* (my dear Camille) and closes, *Votre vieille Amie* (your old friend), with a careful paragraph of French in between. It is all very intriguing. Was Camille

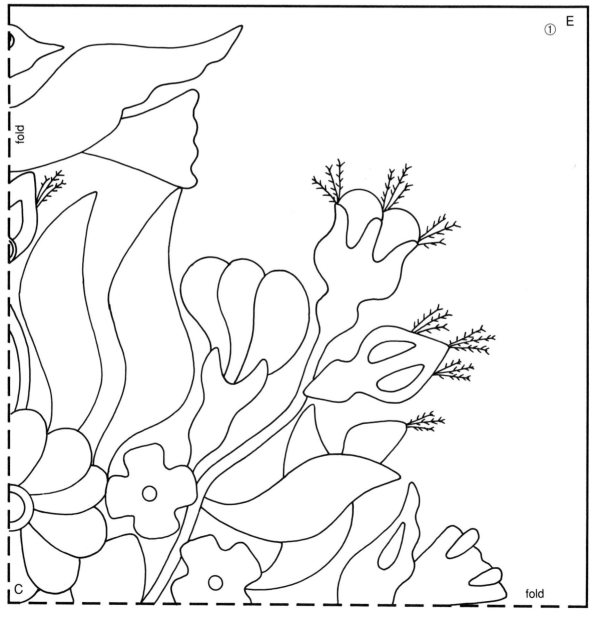

PATTERN #47: *"Bouquet avec Trois Oiseaux"**

Second Page

French? Were these schoolgirls who had all learned French together? More mysteries, and this time compounded by a foreign tongue!

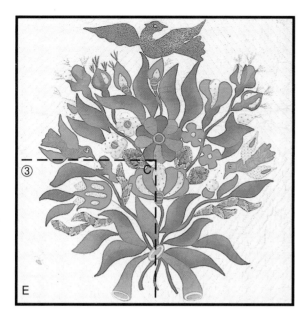

PATTERN #47: *"Bouquet avec Trois Oiseaux"**

Third Page

PATTERN #47: *"Bouquet avec Trois Oiseaux"**

Fourth Page

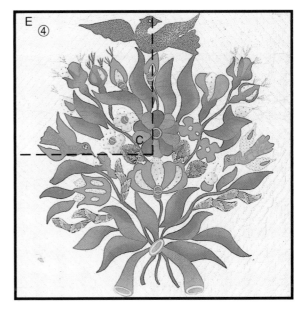

PATTERN #48: "Lyre with Wreath, Bird, and Crown"*

Type: Classic "Baltimore"

To make this block, refer to *Volume I*, Lessons 5, 7, 9, or 10. See also Appendix I in this book.

Detail: Quilt #2 in the Color Section.

This perfectly beautiful block seems imbued with symbolic intent. The instrument here seems to be not a lyre, but a harp, perhaps the Sacred Harp, the emblem of All Music in Honor of God. An ancient instrument, the harp goes back to the Mesopotamian cradle of civilization and to ancient Egypt. In Norse mythology, the harp was the emblem of a ladder between Earth and Heaven and heroes asked to be buried with it, for that reason. This harp, with its intimations of immortality, would seem to have a hero's crown left on it. The language of flowers tells us that a crown of wild olive is a symbol of Victory, as is a crown of laurel. One could surmise that this crown

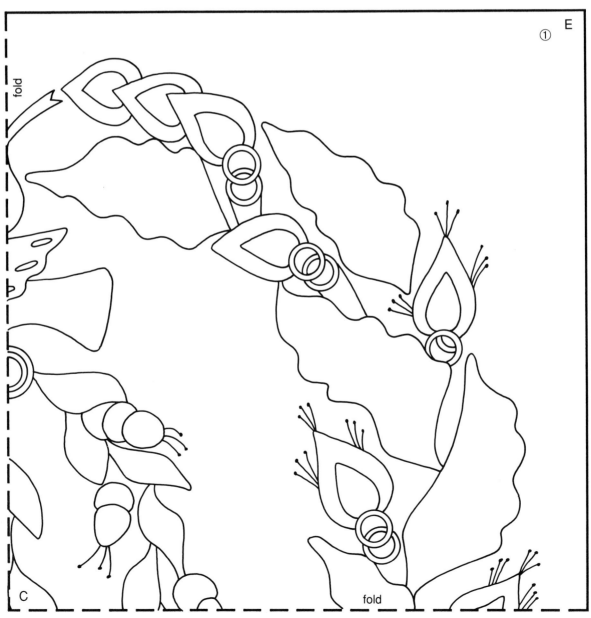

PATTERN #48: "Lyre with Wreath, Bird, and Crown"*

Second Page

might be wild olive, for it is also the sprig in the dove's beak in block D-2 in this quilt. The bird, as a dove, is God's messenger, and stands for Life of the Soul. Exquisite, this block's message is well-clouded by time, but would seem to refer to the fallen heroes represented by the monuments.

Live oak, native to Texas and a symbol on the Texas state seal, seems represented by the outer wreath. If so, this block could honor the fallen Mexican War heroes, Ringgold, Watson, or all. Passionately, though without a word, it echoes the injunction engraved on an adobe wall at the Alamo: "Be silent, friend, here heroes died, to blaze a trail, for other men." In silence, then, this lovely quilt ties present heroes to past. It links Baltimoreans to the nation's service, from Baltimore Harbor to Texas, from the early century to midpoint. Again, a starlike yellow embroidery atop the monument in quilt #3 might possibly

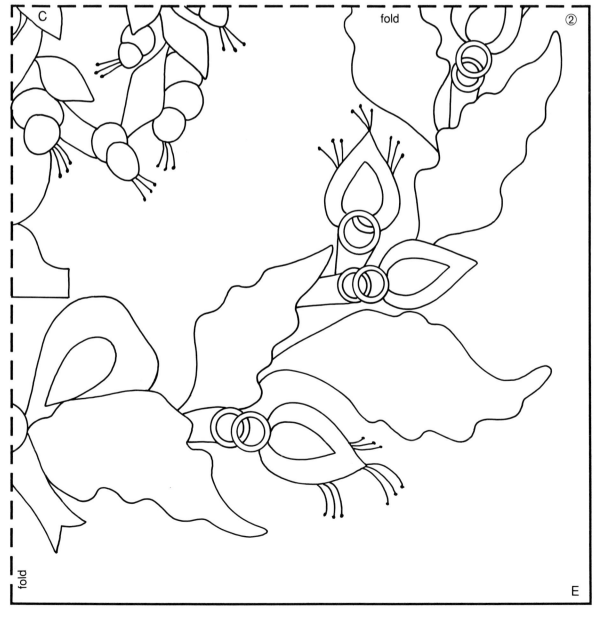

E

PATTERN #48: "Lyre with Wreath, Bird, and Crown"*

Third Page

be the same Masonic compass and square symbol marking the plaque at the Alamo which reads: "Honoring these masons, James Bonham, James Bowie, David Crockett, Almaron Dickerson, William Barrett Travis, and those unidentified masons who gave their lives in the Battle of the Alamo, March 6, 1836."

This block motif is repeated elsewhere in the Baltimore Albums and as with most repeated blocks, the pattern or its placement on the block varies a bit from one quilt to another. To prove the point, and to enrich our offering, you are shown block B-1 from quilt #2 in the photo, and the pattern is drafted from block B-4 in Hezekiah Best's quilt.[19] The bird in the latter is different and the wreath a bit fuller. Yet the fabrics in each block seem similar, and the shapes so close that one has the impression two different patterns were drawn by two different people on the same theme or from the same picture.

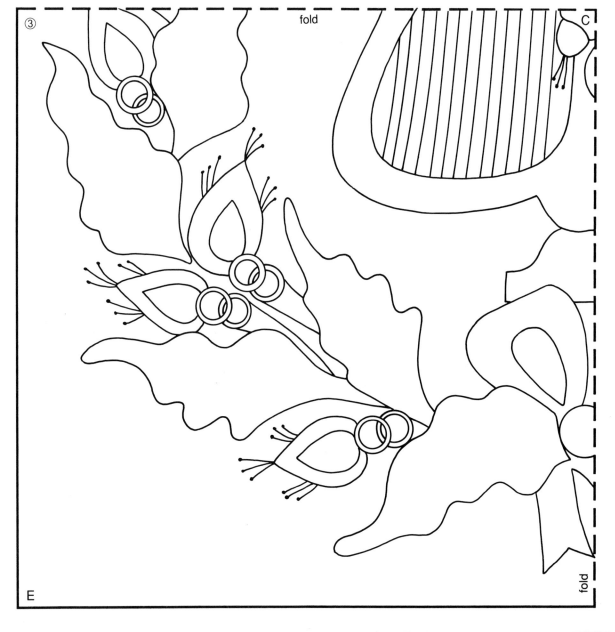

PATTERN #48: "Lyre with Wreath, Bird, and Crown"*

Fourth Page

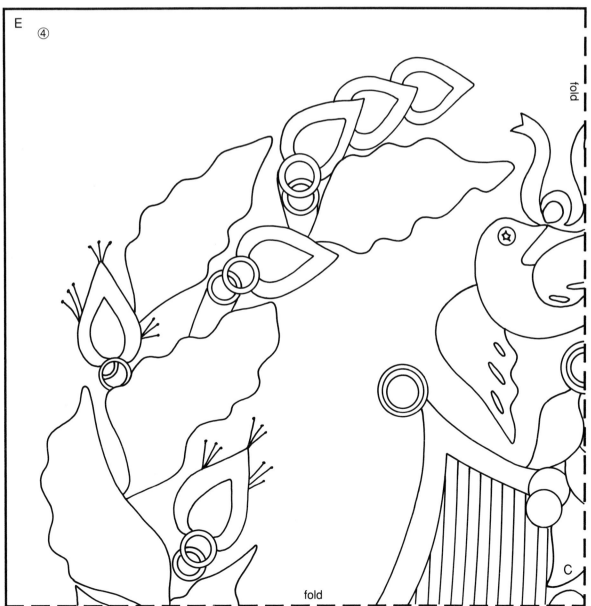

PATTERN #49: "Cornucopia II"*

Type: Classic "Baltimore"

To make this block, refer to *Volume I, Lessons 5, 7,* or *10.* See also Appendix I in this book.

Detail: *Volume I,* quilt #2.

Cornucopias occur frequently in the classic Baltimore Album Quilts. Sometimes they are shown diagonally on the block and make wonderful corner blocks, offering their plenty towards the quilt's center (see *Spoken Without a Word,* p. 60). Sometimes they are filled with fruits, sometimes flowers, sometimes both. And sometimes they appear with acorns thrown in to symbolize Longevity and Immortality. The one patterned here is a particularly beautiful block with the balancing design elements of a fruit and a bird to the left and right of the tip. These square the block off so that it fits in well with other blocks

PATTERN #49: "Cornucopia II"*

Second Page

which are set straight. It fills the block in a similar fashion to upright bouquets and vases of flowers.

Beyond being a lovely neoclassical design motif, the cornucopia was an important Odd Fellow symbol. This at a time when fraternal orders were immensely popular, so much so that many people belonged to several at once. Odd Fellowdom, in the United States, started with Lodge #1 being built in Baltimore in 1819. Possibly most importantly, a women's degree of Odd Fellowdom, the Daughters of Rebekah, was founded in 1851 in Baltimore. Great excitement, meetings in homes, and conceivably fundraising, which may have included the making of quilt blocks, and quilts for sale, preceded the building and dedication of the Crown Rebekah Lodge #1 in Baltimore on Fels Road.

The issue of fraternal symbolism is dealt with in more detail in *Volume II*, but suffice it to say that certain block

PATTERN #49: "Cornucopia II"*

Third Page

motifs that we think of as classic Album Quilt blocks in the uniquely ornate, realistic, Victorian style, designs which include cornucopias and doves bearing an olive branch within an elaborate wreath, are Odd Fellow/ Rebekah symbols and may have been being used intentionally as such.

A second reason why cornucopias may have held the limelight is pointed out by Edna Barth.[20] Though we grew up on tales of the Pilgrims' famous harvest feast of 1621, few of us are aware that Thanksgiving did not become a national holiday until centuries later. Mrs. Sarah Josepha Hale, editor of the magazine *Godey's Lady's Book*, and probably well-known by name at least to many makers of the Baltimore-area Album Quilts, felt that a day of Thanksgiving should be celebrated by the whole nation at one time. For twenty years she urged this through her articles, letters to presidents and governors,

PATTERN #51: "Symbolic Fountain"*

Second Page

Union, started in 1826, held its first national convention in Philadelphia in 1833.

Increasingly, I read the symbolism of fraternal orders in these classic quilts. Fraternal orders printed charts that were basically teaching tools: each symbol being the "visible sign" of a moral or religious precept. Virtually the same fountain seen in this quilt block appears on the symbolic chart of the Knights Templars, a Masonic order. Temperance was an important element in the teachings of the Freemasons. Beneath the fountain are depicted two gavels which appear on Odd Fellow charts, and which to Masons symbolized the tool that would chip off the rough edges of vice and human foible, as one sought self-perfection. The clasped hands, too, were an Odd Fellows and a Freemason symbol, being a visible image or reminder of giving and receiving signs of recognition.

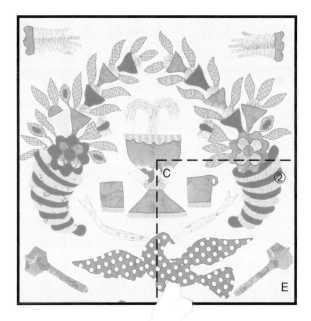

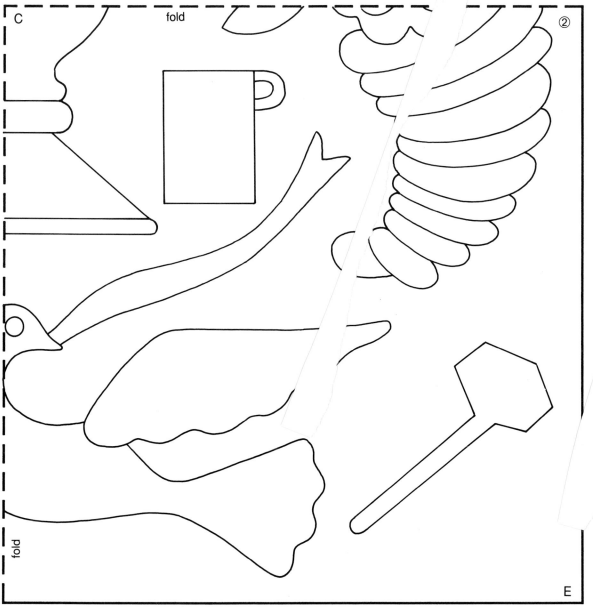

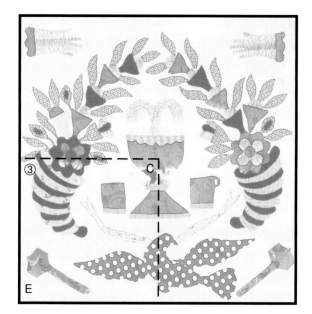

PATTERN #51: "Symbolic Fountain"*

Third Page

It is interesting to note that "The Fountain" is an antique quilting pattern as well. Ruth E. Finley shows an old template for this in *Old Patchwork Quilts and the Women Who Made Them* (plate 76). It is from a set of patterns "owned and used by my grandmother and her mother before her.... There was 'Fountain' wall-paper, 'Fountain' chintz, and 'Fountain' china. Doubtless there was also 'Fountain' quilting." Counting back three generations would place Mrs. Finley's heirloom quilting templates firmly into prime temperance movement times.

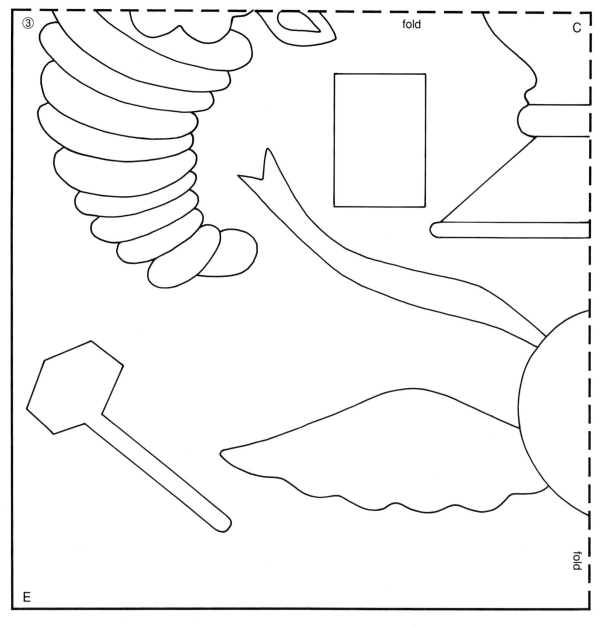

PATTERN #51: "Symbolic Fountain"*

Fourth Page

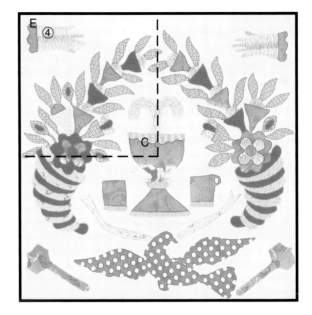

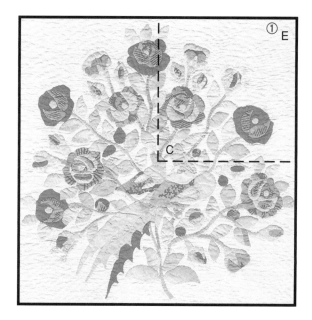

PATTERN #52: "Tropical Bird in a Bush"*

Type: Classic "Baltimore"

To make this block, refer to *Volume I*, Lessons 1 or 2, 5 or 10. See also Appendix I in this book.

Detail: Quilt #4 in the Color Section.

This is a bird of a very fancy feather in a most elegant rosebush replete with cutwork appliqué roses. As the eighteenth century had been the era of flower illustrators, so the nineteenth was that of bird illustrators and the greatest was American resident John James (Jean Jacques) Audubon (1785–1851). He published *Birds of America* serially beginning in 1827. Upon completion, it contained 1,065 lifesize hand-colored figures of American birds. Sold by subscription only, the first edition of the folio cost a hefty $1,000. One can imagine the excitement, then, when a "miniature" edition (a seven-volume set!) was published in the 1840s for just $100. *The Heyday of Natural*

PATTERN #52: "Tropical Bird in a Bush"*

Second Page

History reports that it sold 1,200 copies as against 150 for the first edition. By the 1860s, repeated, ever cheaper printings put it well within the budget of middle-class American families.

Audubon's book was of North American birds, but there were many other, well-illustrated naturalist books available at a moderate price from the 1840s on. Multiple titles dealt with tropical flora and fauna, from the expensive *Orchidaceae* of Mexico and Guatemala to John Gould's fourteen folio books of 2,999 hand-colored lithographs, two especially popular ones being *Toucans* and *Hummingbirds*. Lynn Barber elucidates the Victorian mind a bit when she writes, "Buying a book merely for the sake of its pretty pictures was considered vaguely immoral, or at any rate extravagant, but if those pictures happened to illustrate important and revealing truths about Nature— if they were in fact illustrations of God's benevolent

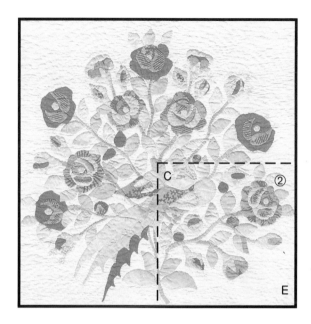

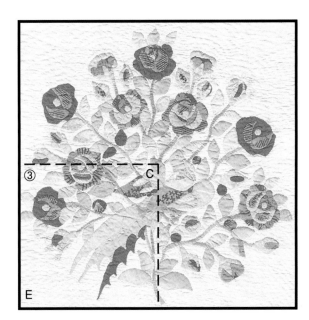

PATTERN #52: "Tropical Bird in a Bush"*

Third Page

Design—then their purchase was justified. Publishers were quick to exploit this important motive, and it is rare to find a natural history book after the 1840s without any illustrations" (*Ibid.*, p. 85).

One might with a clear conscience, then, acquire the work of Audubon's rival, Charles Waterton. This Briton authored the 1825 best-seller, *Wanderings in South America*, which "evoked all the most desirable ingredients—exoticism, adventure and the Great Unknown. Wandering, preferably where white man's foot had never trod, was then in vogue and South America was agreed to be the most exciting possible place to wander" (*Ibid.*, p. 99). Having sought to convey a bit more of our Album quiltmakers' passion for Natural History, we leave the exact folio and lithograph which may have been the model for this gorgeous block's bird for a diligent future researcher to discover!

PATTERN #52: "Tropical Bird in a Bush"*

Fourth Page

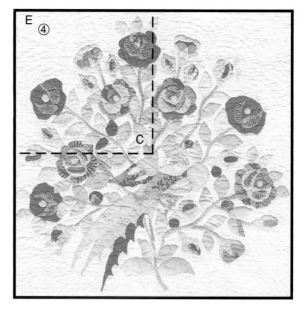

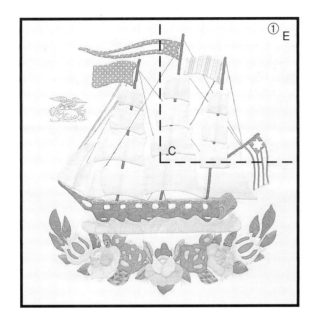

PATTERN #53: "Clipper Ship"*

Type: The ship is Classic Baltimore, captured exquisitely by Sylvia Pickell.

To make this block, refer to *Volume I*, Lessons 5, 9, or 10. See also Appendix I in this book.

A magnificent clipper ship, the *Ann McKim*, like the one in this block, was built in Baltimore and launched in 1833. That event ushered in the era of the great clipper ships. By 1840, clippers, a rather ill-defined term (possibly derived from the expression "going at a fast clip") were skyrocketing in popularity on both sides of the Atlantic. Already, smaller ships of the genre were known as "Baltimore Clippers," and such impetus was given to the class by the California gold rush that 160 clippers were launched in four years to carry some 90,000 people west. American families—Bell, Hall, Steers, Webb, Collier, McKay, and Magoun—built clipper ships, and the Osgood, Marshall, Trask, Woodhouse, Delano, De Puyster, and Russell

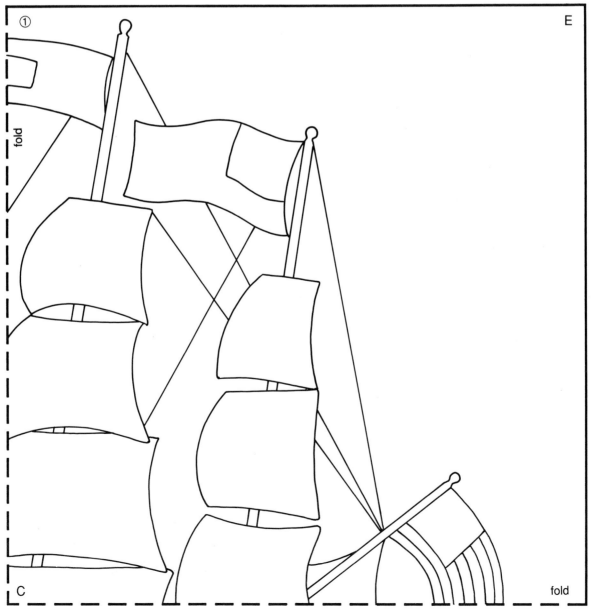

PATTERN #53: "Clipper Ship"*

Second Page

families provided many captains for the ships. After 1845, freight rates dropped and American shipbuilders switched to a smaller, less expensive "modified clipper" which never equalled the speed (up to 18 knots) of the original "extreme clipper." Clippers plied the high seas predominately between the eastern United States' ports and China. Beyond the gold rushes, and the opium and slave trades, the Chinese tea trade offered a potent motive for speed on the water. Because the fresh tea's flavor was perishable in a ship's hold, merchants offered annual prizes for the fastest delivery of the season's crop. *The Cutty Sark* (built in 1869) holds the record, 363 miles covered in one day in the annual tea-run race.

With her hull characteristically painted in bands of black and white, with dummy portholes painted in black, with great numbers of billowing sails and a long, sharp bow, the clipper ship was stunningly picturesque.

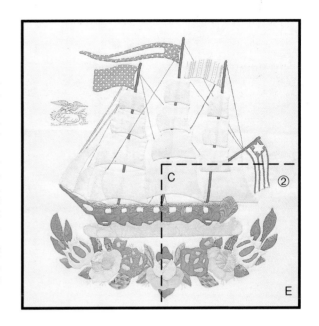

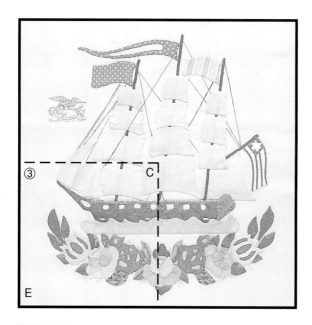

PATTERN #53: "Clipper Ship"*

Third Page

And what of the American flag she flew? In this block's original, the stars on the flag are shown by a five-petaled printed flower. More often they are depicted in the pattern of one great five-pointed star. This flag, the "Great Star Flag," was called by Oliver Wendell Holmes the "starry flower of liberty" and its petaled star shape (which was to become the flag of the American Merchant Marine) held sway from 1818 to the end of the Civil War. Though legislated guidelines for the precise design of the American flag were not set down until two decades into the twentieth century, the Great Star Flag in its manifold varieties was longer our flag than any since. It appeared in 1782 on the Great Seal of the United States and to this day the design appears above our national symbol on the dollar bill.

This magnificent Clipper Ship block is one of a small handful of gorgeous oceangoing vessels in the Baltimore

PATTERN #53: "Clipper Ship"*

Fourth Page

Album Quilts. Their manufacture reflected the mid-nineteenth-century shipbuilding revolution, then well underway in America. The dynamic changes (in construction, from wood to steel, and in propulsion, from sails to steam) in the mid-nineteenth century saw America dominate world commerce and the City of Baltimore prospered thereby.

Briton Samual Cunard founded the transatlantic Cunard Steamship line in 1840. Charles Dickens crossed the Atlantic to America on the *Britannia* in 1842, a two-cylinder side-lever paddle engine. On October 10, 1845, Secretary of the Navy George Bancroft oversaw the opening of the Annapolis Naval Academy at Fort Severn, not far from Baltimore. And the U.S. brought out its first transatlantic steamers in 1847 to run between New York and Bremen. Pride in all this progress is reflected in the Baltimore Album Quilts.

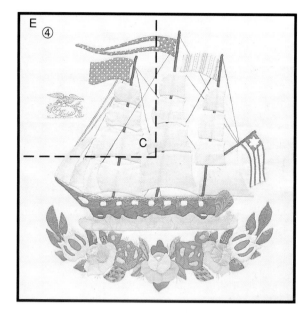

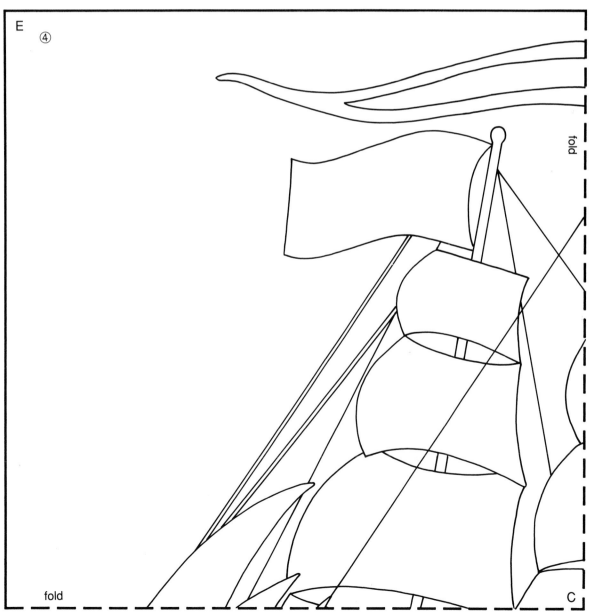

PATTERN #54: "Peacock Pastorale"*

Type: Classic "Baltimore"

To make this block, refer to *Volume I*, Lessons 1 or 2, 5 or 10. See also Appendix I in this book.

Detail: *Volume I*, quilt #2.

The peacock in a lush bush is a recurring motif in the classic Baltimore Album Quilts. In my experience, it is mainly done in the ornate, more realistic, Victorian style, rather than in the sort of simplified version of block C-5 of quilt #3. You can see other versions of this same block in the Metropolitan's Baltimore Album Quilt (photo #26 in *Volume I*); in the quilt inscribed "To John and Rebecca Chamberlain" (shown in *Volume II*); and in quilt #2 in the Color Section. The slight variations among these three are part of the evidence which could mean different makers working in virtually the same style.

PATTERN #54: "Peacock Pastorale"*

Second Page

What is intriguing to me is that all three blocks could be reflecting the same design source. But the drafting of their shapes, fabric choices, and the layout of the motifs within the block all differ. And why peacocks? To begin with, no other bird calls for quite such an exotic display of fabric feathers. Beyond this, peacocks symbolize Immortality, and the "eyes" on its feathers represent the All-Seeing Eye of God. The peacock here is perched near an egg-filled nest, a sure omen of Fruitfulness and, in some cultures, Good Luck. This block in all its modest complexity would be an excellent one on which to try out the appliqué approach outlined in Appendix I.

PATTERN #54: "Peacock Pastorale"*

Third Page

PATTERN #54: "Peacock Pastorale"*

Fourth Page

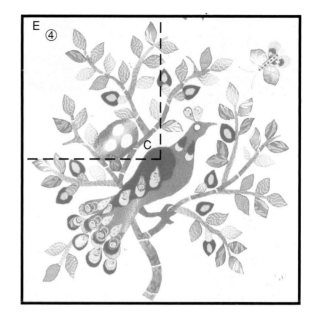

PATTERN #55: "Wreath and Dove II"*

Type: Classic "Baltimore"

To make this block, refer to *Volume I*, Lessons 5, 7, or 10. See also Appendix I in this book.

Detail: Quilt #2.

In *Spoken Without a Word*, I speculated about what sort of bird this gracefully crested creature might be. Increasingly, I believe this is a stylization of a dove, not with a crest but with a little "fillip" to its head feathers. The body, the characteristic pose as God's messenger to Noah with the wild olive sprig in its beak, and its prevalence in these quilts would all seem to confirm this. The dove was a favorite symbol of the Daughters of Rebekah, the women Odd Fellows.

The Odd Fellows Monitor and Guide[23] says of the Dove, "This emblem presents to us important lessons for practice in life.... The cooing dove is the embodiment of

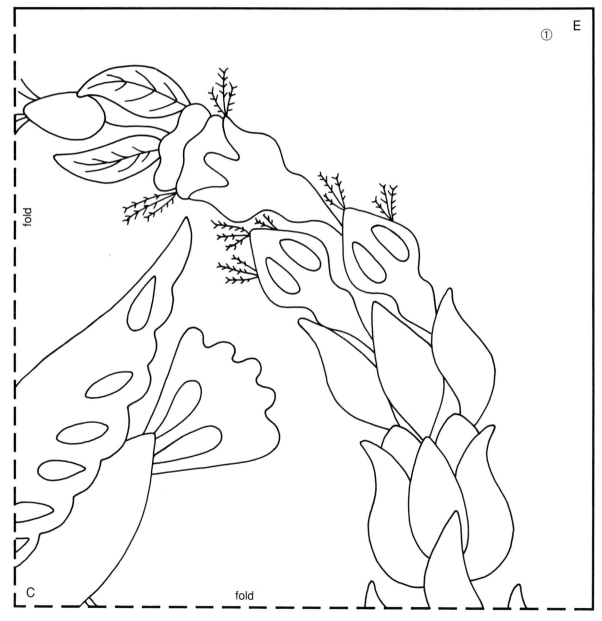

PATTERN #55: "Wreath and Dove II"*

Second Page

innocence and seems to injure nothing.... This emblem may also remind us of the Holy Spirit that descended, and in the form of a dove sat upon the head of the Savior as he stood upon the bank of the far-famed Jordan after he had been baptized by John.... This emblem tells us that we too may have the visits of that comforting messenger typified by Noah's dove. Yes, we may learn in its blessed influences on our hearts that the waters of Jehovah's wrath are assuaged, and that in the salvation provided, so beautifully typified by the ark, the offender may be reconciled with the offended."[24]

The dove, then, is tied to Noah and his ark as well, and this brings us full-circle back to the Masons who would seem a rather important factor in quilt #2. The dove could symbolize the "Ark and Dove" degree, formerly of Royal Arch Masonry. Masons use the dove only in this context, though.

PATTERN #55: "Wreath and Dove II"*

Third Page

Taken simply at face value, this is a beautiful block which any of us would be thrilled to put in our Album.

PATTERN #55: "Wreath and Dove II"*

Fourth Page

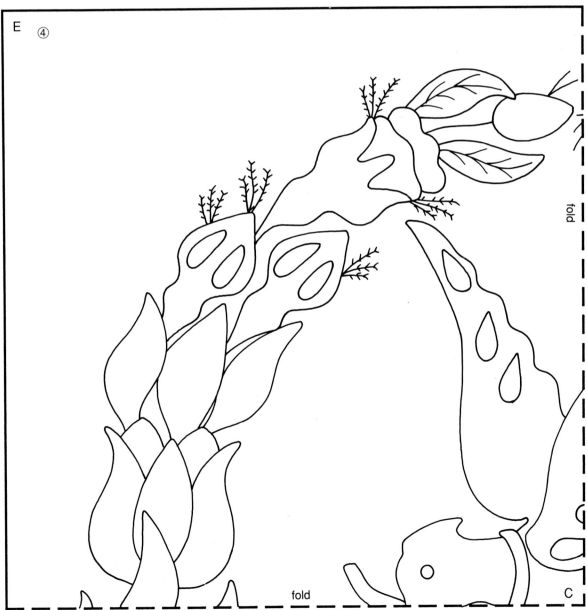

PATTERN #56: "Four-Ribbon Wreath"*

Type: Classic "Baltimore"

To make this block, refer to *Volume I*, Lessons 5, 7, 9 or 10. See also Appendix I in this book.

Detail: *Volume I*, quilt #2.

In looking closely at sets of the classic Baltimore Album Quilts in *Volume II*, you will see how in certain quilts open floral wreaths have become very important design elements which organize the quilt and give it a secondary design, adding yet one more level of richness to the genre. This pattern provides an elegant open wreath for such a use. The decorative concept of ribbon-tied garlands of flowers which is the basis for this block, goes back centuries in Western art. Averill Colby in *Patchwork* tells us that the triple bow-tied festoon was used by Chippendale for his Ormulu [*sic*] mounts.

PATTERN #56: "Four-Ribbon Wreath"*

Second Page

What seems significant to me in this and numerous very similar blocks, is that the floral medallion seems to form a star or compass in the wreath's center. One hypothesis might be that the symbolism of the star or compass was intended, but a designer chose to render it in flowers rather than depicting a more traditional star. One could argue with equal conviction that these ladies were on the lookout for appealing objects to fill the center of their wreaths and that this flower arrangement filled the bill! In which case, perhaps this floral star medallion is no more and no less symbolic than the birds (Life of the Soul), squirrels (Thrift), white roses (Eternal love), lyres (Divine Music), and in one case, "the bricklayer's home," which fill other open wreaths in other classic blocks.

Stars mean Divine Guidance, an appropriate wish for almost any Album Quilt. They may also have had more

PATTERN #56: "Four-Ribbon Wreath"*

Third Page

specific symbolism at times in these quilts, such as the Lone Star for Texas, or the five-pointed star of the Odd Fellows, or the six-pointed Seal of Solomon of the Masons. The compass is also an emblem of Guidance.

PATTERN #56: "Four-Ribbon Wreath"*

Fourth Page

PATTERNS, continued

Pattern #1, continued from page 22

because of its sentiment and because it serves as a memorial to the Methodist influence in the Baltimore Album Quilts. Dr. Dunton, in *Old Quilts*, points out the strong Methodist hand in many, though probably not all, of these quilts. Numerous names from these Baltimore quilts are recorded in mid-nineteenth-century Methodist class lists and in family genealogies connected to these quilts. Quilts were often inscribed to Methodist class leaders and ministers and there are even picture blocks of churches.

Brought to the United States in the 1760s, Methodism first took root in New York, New Jersey, Pennsylvania, and Maryland. The Church in America followed founder John Wesley's precept of people gathered into classes for Christian fellowship under the guidance of a lay leader. Several points seem pertinent to the Album Quilts. First, the weekly class system meant that while one attended one's regular class weekly, on a given Sunday a Baltimorean might attend any Methodist church in the Baltimore Conference.[1] This institutionalized mixing of great numbers of Methodists might help explain how particular quilt sets and block patterns, fabrics, and styles in the Baltimore Album Quilts could be spread within the church and community as a whole on such a scale.

Second, Methodism in the mid-nineteenth century had a heightened social conscience expressed by communal concern over social evils, "sweated labor, poverty, and squalor." The Album Quilts would surely reflect some of these concerns. From its beginning, American Methodism had a missionary purpose as well and sent its first missionaries to Africa in 1833, to South America in 1835, and to China in 1847. In *Old Quilts* (p. 153), Dr. Dunton notes three missionary-connected repeat block Album Quilts, though the denomination they represent is uncertain. One, of repeated fleurs-de-lis, is inscribed, in part, "Presented to Rev. Mr. Minor by/the Young Ladies of/Thorndale Seminary./The names of the contributors being written on the quilt." Another square reads "Rev. Mr. Minor of the African Mission."

The Baltimore Albums may signal pro- or anti-slavery sympathies by the presence or absence of the "Phrygian" or "freedom" cap in the eagle blocks. In that context, it's interesting to note that Maryland was a slaveholding state, whose citizens were severely divided on the issue. After the 1844 General Conference opened the way for a pro-slavery Methodist Episcopal Church South, the Baltimore Conference joined the Northern, anti-slavery, Methodist churches. Yet more insight into who made these quilts might possibly be gathered through studying *The Ladies Repository and Gathering of the West*, a women's literary magazine from the Methodist publishing house.

The Methodist emphasis on a life guided by love was fervently espoused as well by fraternal orders, including the Masons and the Odd Fellows, whose symbols seem so pervasive in these quilts (and a topic discussed in detail in *Volume II*). From whatever sources, the very ethos of fellowship and love, love of God, love of Country, love of friends, pervades the Album Quilts.

Pattern #6, continued from page 27

symbolic meanings—hearts speak of Love, Devotion, or Charity. And as for the swans in this pattern? They symbolize Andersen's fairy tale, "The Ugly Duckling." This endearing story promised hope to us in our own gawky youth, and was no doubt autobiographical. Raised painfully poor and self-conscious about his appearance,

Andersen the adult was the world's most widely published author of his day and hobnobbed with royalty.

Pattern #8, continued from page 29

Dr. Dunton, in *Old Quilts*, points out the strong German influence in these quilts. Baltimore, during the three decades before the Civil War, was the port of entry for thousands of Germans immigrants. Though some earned passage for the return journey aboard Baltimore's cotton and tobacco exporting boats, many stayed in the area, joining Germans of earlier immigrations. It is particularly noteworthy, in connection with the Baltimore Album Quilts, that certain Methodist churches in Baltimore were essentially German churches.

Pattern #9, continued from page 30

pattern may well reflect a strong German influence, like the Pennsylvania Dutch (Pennsylvania *Deutsch*) themselves. Innocently, I did this block all in reverse appliqué. (See notes for Pattern #10.) It would, however, have been more easily done using reverse[2] appliqué (Lesson 3) for the red only, and onlaid appliqué (Lesson 5) for the green.

Pattern #10, continued from page 31

quilt as "Passion Flowers."[3] The passionflower, a name bestowed by the early missionaries in South America, has an intricate and detailed symbology connected with the Passion of Christ. Only one of an estimated 500 species of *passifloraceae* is clearly designated passionfruit. The passionfruit plant has leaves which are "deeply three lobed when mature." Thus what may be depicted in this block and those "Passion Flowers" to which Dunton refers may be another variety of this flowering vine such as *passiflora antioquiensis* which has simple leaves like slim pointed elongated ovals.

Though this block's bloom might in fact have been intended as a passionflower with its thick center and leafy vine, I've named it (both somewhat cautiously and generically) "Red Vases and Red Flowers," placing the emphasis on the four vase-like motifs at the block's center. This central motif, in combination with leaves and flowers, was a theme with extensive variations in classic Album Quilt block design. (For example, see Pattern #11.)

Its Christian analogy alone could explain the repeated presence of the passionflower in the largely Christian Baltimore Album Quilts. In addition, the eighteenth century had been the era of the great botanical illustrators. Botanical prints such as the aqua-tinted engravings of Dr. Robert John Thornton might have graced interiors familiar to these quiltmakers.

Further, botanical expeditions bringing back new specimens would most likely pass through New York or Baltimore. Perhaps it shouldn't surprise us that notable botanical finds seem rather quickly reflected in Album Quilt portraits of the plants themselves: plants such as the Christmas cactus, moss roses (introduced to the U.S. in the 1840s), the passionflower, and ornamental peppers from Mexico. One wonders if some of the ships depicted in the Baltimore Album Quilts might not be carrying scientific specimen-gathering expeditions from the bustling port of Baltimore to tropical America and Australia?

Pattern #11, continued from page 32

however, seem so fond of symbolism, so sympathetic to the tenets of Freemasonry and Odd Fellowdom, that such factors must be seriously considered.

In *Spoken Without a Word*, I named this block after the acanthus flower, another neoclassical favorite, based on a photograph of the acanthus leaf and a verbal description of this succulent plant which has a bract at the bloom's base. Most classic and neoclassic representations of the acanthus leaf are more curvacious and undulating. This prim, tight version, however, looks at least equally close to the botanical original.

Pattern #12, continued from page 33

fascinating article on this plant in *American Horticulture* (December 1988). She adds, "Homes of yesteryear were perfect for growing the Christmas cactus. Heat from corner stoves left areas nearest windows cooler; lamplight did not brighten the room's periphery. The aerial roots sprouting between stem segments, originally used for clinging to its native host, absorbed moisture created by cool air. There great-grandmother left her plant, protected year-round from atmospheric extremes."

Pattern #13, continued from page 34

Because fraternal order symbolism seems so important in these quilts, mention should be made of the importance the Masons saw in the square and in geometry in general. For Masons, Geometry, "the first and noblest of the sciences," symbolized Symmetry and Order, and therefore the Divine Plan. They speak of non-Masons as "unmade masons" or "imperfect ashlars," those rough-hewn stones in nature's imperfect state. The goal of a Mason is to smooth off these rough edges and to become a "block" (by self-perfection) that will help build God's temple. The square as a Masonic tool is an important symbol, as are the three squares of the Forty-Seventh Problem of Euclid which "teaches masons to be lovers of the arts and sciences."[4]

Pattern #14, continued from page 35

the folded circle rosebuds from Lesson 6: 3½" diameter circles for the outside rosebuds; 2⅜" circles for the inside corner rosebuds, and 2½" circles for the inner center rosebuds.

Pattern #15, continued from page 36

quilts, and the grape in general symbolizes the Blood of Christ in the Eucharist, while the wild grape symbolizes Charity. Green leaves symbolize Hope Renewed. Christ is referred to as The True Vine; there is also The Church where God is the Keeper of the Vineyard.

Several other Biblical references may also illuminate the import of grapes and grapevines in Christian iconography and thus in these often overtly religious quilts. In the King James Version, we read in Psalms (chapter 128, verse 3) that "Thy wife shall be as a fruitful vine by the sides of thine house: thy children like olive plants round about thy table." And in the Gospels (John, chapter 15, verse 5), "I am the vine, ye are the branches."

Pattern #19, continued from page 40

greenery is stitched with green wool. If you use the technique in Appendix I, try stuffing the flowers by slitting the back after the appliqué is complete. This will reduce distortion. While the pattern simply suggests the embroidery, you can best see the actual stitches used by looking through a good magnifying glass.

Pattern #20, continued from page 41

poking his bill into a flower. Below is Mrs. John Mann, Exeter Street, Baltimore." Dena Katzenberg in *Baltimore*

Album Quilts (p. 84) records this inscription as "Mrs. John Mann, Eutaw Street, Baltie."

With the circle speaking of never-ending, Eternal Things, and the rose of Love, I've long thought this could serve as an "in memoriam" block to honor someone who has died. One might borrow this lovely phrase from another classic Baltimore Album Quilt: "May I twine a wreath for thee, Sacred to love and memory."[5]

Pattern #21, continued from page 43

women of the town organized a ball in his honor. A pretty story is told of the Marquis looking disconsolate in spite of all the beauty and gaiety around him. Being asked the reason he replied that he could not help thinking about his poor ill-clad soldiers. A hint was all that was needed. The townspeople at once came through...a committee of ladies set to work making 500 'garments' for Lafayette's troops."[6]

An elder statesman, his triumphal farewell tour of America in 1824 brought untrammeled adulation. He was well-loved both as a man and as a hero, but now also as a symbol of the American Revolution, which was only gradually receding into history. Certainly a symbol of French Republicanism, the fleur-de-lis (particularly when embellished, as here, with laurel) may well have memorialized Lafayette, "the man to whose devotion the country was so largely indebted for the independence which it had secured."[7]

Pattern #31, continued from page 62

additional information.) There seems evidence, though, that what is depicted here is a bough of cherries in a heart-shaped wreath. For some ideas on why this might be so, see the discussion of quilt #3, block C-3, in "Part One: The Quiltmakers." Cherries mean Sweet Character, Good Deeds, and are combined here with hearts (Love, Devotion or Charity) and bluebirds (Life of the Soul). In Christian iconography, blue means Truth.

This version of a wreathed vine with, possibly, highly stylized cherry leaves, cherries, and bluebirds, is often repeated. This is a particularly charming version of it, our model here having been made by Shirley Bertolino Hedman. Blocks similar to Version I can be seen in quilt #3 in the Color Section and in *Volume I*, quilt #4.

Pattern #45, continued from page 127

Victory, Prowess in Battle. Of these German social clubs, the Turners and the choral societies of the lower classes were adamantly pro-Union. "At the outbreak of hostilities the Baltimore Turners were so closely allied with the Union cause that their hall was attacked by Southern sympathizers. They volunteered in large numbers for service with the Northern armies. On the other hand, the wealthy German merchants favored the South where they had many close business ties."[18]

Pattern #49, continued from page 143

them and for them: "This, then, is our aim: to diffuse and make popular the simple but efficient lessons of home happiness and goodness. Much is in the power of the mothers and wives of our land to make happy families, and thus insure a happy nation."

NOTES

[1] Conversation with Rev. Edwin Schell, Executive Secretary, United Methodist Historical Society.

[2] I believe I misunderstood Averil Colby's use of the term "inlaid appliqué" and passed that misunderstanding on in Lessons 1 and 3 in *Volume I*. Aside from wishing, of course, to convey correct information, I was a bit disappointed to find this the case, for "inlaid" paired with "onlaid" seemed so well-spoken. The term "onlaid" remains as conveyed, but a very clear description of what inlaid appliqué consists of appears in *Encyclopedia of Victorian Needlework* (p. 8): "Appliqué is divided into Inlaid and Onlaid, and from these heads spring many adaptations of the work. To make: Carefully design the pattern upon a foundation material, and lay these in to the foundation without a margin or selvedge overlapping either to the front or back of the work. Stitch them into position, and conceal the joins and lines of stitches by couching down a line of gold cord, narrow ribbon, of floss silk over those places. Great nicety is required in the cutting out and fitting into place of the various pieces, and sewing them down. The materials used in Inlaid Appliqué should match as to substance, or a thinner one be backed with linen when used with a thicker, otherwise the finished work will strain and wrinkle. Inlaid Appliqué was much used in Italy in the eleventh century." This is, in fact, what Averil Colby seems also to have been describing, leaving us to revert to the terms "onlaid appliqué" and "reverse appliqué" for what we have been doing all along in Lesson 3!

[3] William Rush Dunton, Jr., *Old Quilts*, published by the author, Catonsville, Md., 1946, p. 31. Dr. Dunton (1868–1966) was a psychiatrist (with a passion for quilts) and a founding father of occupational therapy; he seems to have been the first person to write systematically about the Maryland Album Quilts. Dunton appears to be the originator of several theories about these quilts and their makers, theories which have come under close scrutiny in recent years and are treated in *Volume II*. His unpublished *Notebooks*, in the Baltimore Museum of Art, contain the rejection letters he received when trying to get his manuscript published. Muttering to friends that he could ill-afford it, he self-published 2,000 copies of *Old Quilts* in 1946. Now a rare and pricey book, *Old Quilts* is not even listed among his publications in the page-long writeup on him in the *National Cyclopedia of Biography*. Ironically noting how times have changed, my friend Nancy Smith commented, "His quilt book, *Old Quilts*, is stolen from libraries. His occupational therapy books are not."

[4] Barbara Franco, *Masonic Symbolism in American Decorative Arts*, Scottish Rite Museum, New York, 1976, p. 50.

[5] Dena Katzenberg, *Baltimore Album Quilts*, Baltimore Museum of Art, Baltimore, Md., 1981, p. 100. Quilt #15, accession #46.159.

[6] Francis Beirne, *The Amiable Baltimoreans*, Johns Hopkins University Press, Baltimore, Md., 1984.

[7] James McSherry, *History of Maryland*, Baltimore Book Company, Baltimore, Md., 1904, p. 330.

[8] Edna Barth, *Hearts, Cupids, and Red Roses*, Seabury Press, New York, 1974, p. 49.

[9] *Ibid.*, p. 52, quoting James Boyle O'Reilly.

[10] *Ibid.*, pp. 42–44.

[11] *Ibid.*, p. 42.

[12] Edna Barth, *Turkeys, Pilgrims, and Indian Corn*, Seabury Press, New York, 1975, p. 92.

[13] Jeremy Cross, *The True Masonic Chart*, New Haven, 1824, p. 38.

[14] The original quilt is shown in Bishop's *New Discoveries in American Quilts* (Dutton, New York, 1975). Though the quilt is labeled in that book as from "Lancaster, Pennsylvania," some authorities question this origin. Often what is passed down as the origin of a quilt is where it was purchased, probably in this century. There are examples of this type of quilt in Maryland, in Delaware, and probably in Pennsylvania.

[15] *Quilt Digest*, 1983, p. 36.

[16] One of these blocks is in *Volume I*, photo #26, block B-1, the other is in the Penn-Magruder quilt in *Volume III*, the third, this one.

[17] Beirne, *The Amiable Baltimoreans*, pp. 204–205.

[18] *Ibid.*, p. 206.

[19] Katzenberg, *Baltimore Album Quilts*, quilt #7. The pattern is taken from a block in the quilt inscribed "Balt" and "Balto" and with the dates 1845, 1846, and 1847. It was made for Rev. Hezekiah Best and is in the collection of the Lovely Lane Museum of the United Methodist Historical Society in Baltimore.

[20] *Ibid.*

[21] Dunton, *Old Quilts*, Plate 18, pp. 80–86. The center block is of a house enclosed by an ornate, realistic, Victorian broken wreath of flowers. Above it is a heavily drawn scroll inscribed "Mary E. Gray," and below it "The Bricklayer's Home 1851." This block intrigues me, for it and several others in the quilt appear to be in the ornate Victorian style which Dunton connects (in his unpublished *Notebooks*) to Mary Evans, married name Ford. Dena Katzenberg, in *Baltimore Album Quilts*, tells us Mary Evans's father, Daniel Evans, was a bricklayer, and that Mary married John Ford of New York in 1873. Mary would have been about 43 at that time and I have always wondered if this Mary E. Gray inscribed above the bricklayer's house might not reflect an earlier marriage for Mary.

[22] Charles Titus, *The Old Line State: Her Heritage*, Tidewater, Cambridge, Md., 1971, p. 53.

[23] Rev. T. G. Beharrell, *Odd Fellows Monitor and Guide*, Robert Douglass, Indianapolis, 1878, pp. 61–63.

[24] *Ibid.*

Bibliography

HISTORY AND DESIGN BACKGROUND

Barber, Lynn. *The Heyday of Natural History*. Doubleday, New York, 1980.

Beirne, Francis. *The Amiable Baltimoreans*. Johns Hopkins University Press, Baltimore, Md., 1984.

Bickham, George. *The Universal Penman*. (Originally published by George Bickham, London, circa 1740–41.) Dover, New York, 1954.

Bordes, Marilyn. *Twelve Great Quilts from the American Wing*. Metropolitan Museum of Art, New York, 1974.

Brackman, Barbara. "Buds and Blossoms: Nineteenth-Century Album Patterns." *Quilter's Newsletter Magazine*, #213, June 1989, pp. 24–26.

Brown, Becky. "A Shared Treasure: The Penn-Magruder Family Baltimore Album Quilt." *American Quilter*, Summer 1988, pp. 12–13.

Caulfeild, Sophia Frances Anne, and Saward, Blanche. *Encyclopedia of Victorian Needlework, Volumes I and II*. (Originally published in 1882 as *The Dictionary of Needlework: An Encyclopedia of Artistic, Plain, and Fancy Needlework*.) Dover, New York, 1972.

Chittenden, Fred J., editor. T*he Royal Horticultural Society Dictionary of Gardening, A Practical and Scientific Encyclopaedia of Horticulture*. Second edition. Clarendon Press, Oxford, 1956; corrected and reprinted, 1965.

Colby, Averil. *Patchwork*. B. T. Botsford, Ltd., London, 1973.

Cunz, D. *The Maryland Germans, A History*. Princeton University Press, Princeton, N.J., 1948.

Dunton, William Rush, Jr. *Notebooks* (unpublished). In the Baltimore Museum of Art, Baltimore, Md.

Dunton, William Rush, Jr. *Old Quilts*. Published by the author, Catonsville, Md., 1946.

Federal Writers' Project, Works Progress Administration. *Washington, D.C.: A Guide to the Nation's Capital*. Hastings House, New York, 1942.

Finley, Ruth. *Old Patchwork Quilts and the Women Who Made Them*. Lippincott, Philadelphia, 1929; reprinted by C. T. Branford Company, Newton Centre, Mass.,1983.

Hillstrom, Judith. "The Christmas Cactus." *American Horticulture Magazine*, Dec. 1988, pp. 38–40.

Jones, Owen. *The Grammar of Ornament: All 100 Color Plates from the Folio Edition of the Great Victorian Scrapbook of Historic Design*. (First published in England, 1856.) Portland House, New York, 1986.

Katzenberg, Dena. *Baltimore Album Quilts*. Baltimore Museum of Art, Baltimore, Md., 1981.

Laury, Jean Ray, and The California Heritage Quilt Project. *Ho For California*. Dutton, New York, 1990.

Lavitt, Wendy, and Weissman, Judith Reiter. *Labors of Love: America's Textiles and Needlework, 1650–1930*. Knopf, New York, 1987.

McSherry, James. *History of Maryland*. Baltimore Book Company, Baltimore, Md., 1904.

Nelson, Cyril, editor. *The Quilt Engagement Calendar*. Dutton, New York, 1983, 1984, 1985, 1987, 1988.

Orlofsky, Patsy and Myron. *Quilts in America*. McGraw-Hill, New York, 1974.

Rae, Janet. *The Quilts of the British Isles*. Dutton, New York, 1987.

Ring, Betty. *American Needlework Treasures, Samples, and Silk Embroideries from the Collection of Betty Ring*. Dutton, New York, 1987.

Rumford, Beatrix T., and Weekley, Carolyn J. *Treasures of American Folk Art: from the Abby Aldrich Rockefeller Folk Art Center*. Little, Brown, Boston, 1989.

Schlesinger, Arthur M., Jr., editor. *The Almanac of American History*. Putnam, New York, 1983.

Sienkiewicz, Elly. "Album Quilts and Victorian Inkings." *Traditional Quiltworks*, February/March/April 1989, pp. 27–34.

_____. *Baltimore Beauties and Beyond: Studies in Classic Album Quilt Appliqué, Volume I*. C&T Publishing, Lafayette, Calif., 1989.

_____. "Friendship's Offering." *Quilter's Newsletter Magazine*, #212, May 1989, pp. 32–37.

_____. "My Baltimore Album Quilt Discoveries." *Quilter's Newsletter Magazine*, #202, May 1988, pp. 26–27.

_____. "The Numsen Quilt: Fancy Flowers from Old Baltimore." *Quilter's Newsletter Magazine*, #218, January 1990, pp. 12–15.

_____. *Spoken Without a Word: A Lexicon of Selected Symbols with 24 Patterns from Classic Baltimore Album Quilts*. Published by the author, Washington, D.C., 1983.

_____. "Victorian Album Quilts." *Quilter's Newsletter Magazine*, #217, November/December 1989, pp. 32–34, 70.

_____."The World's Most Valuable Quilt." *Quilting Today*, #12, April, May 1989, pp. 6–7, 48.

Sotheby's, Inc. *Important Americana [catalogue], Sale #5680, January 1988.* Sotheby's, New York, 1987.

Spencer, Richard Henry, editor. *Genealogical and Memorial Encyclopedia of the State of Maryland. A Record of the Achievement of Her People in the Making of a Commonwealth and the Founding of a Nation.* American Historical Society, New York, 1919.

Titus, Charles. *The Old Line State: Her Heritage.* Tidewater Publishers, Cambridge, Md., 1971.

The United States Capitol Historical Society. *Washington Past and Present, A Guide to the Nation's Capital.* The United States Capitol Historical Society, Washington, D.C., 1983.

_____. *We the People: The Story of the United States Capitol.* The United States Capitol Historical Society, Washington, D.C., 1964.

Wright, Roxa. "Baltimore Friendship Quilt." *Woman's Day*, October 1965.

SYMBOLISM AND SYMBOLISM IN THE CLASSIC ALBUM QUILTS

Barth, Edna. *Hearts, Cupids, and Red Roses: The Story of the Valentine Symbols.* Seabury Press, New York, 1974.

_____. *Holly, Reindeer, and Colored Lights: The Story of the Christmas Symbols.* Seabury Press, New York, 1971.

_____. *Lilies, Rabbits, and Painted Eggs: The Story of the Easter Symbols.* Seabury Press, New York, 1970.

_____. *Shamrocks, Harps, and Shillelaghs: The Story of the St. Patrick's Day Symbols.* Seabury Press, New York, 1977.

_____. *Turkeys, Pilgrims, and Indian Corn: The Story of the Thanksgiving Symbols.* Seabury Press, New York, 1975.

_____. *Witches, Pumpkins, and Grinning Ghosts: The Story of the Halloween Symbols.* Seabury Press, New York, 1974.

Beharrell, Thomas G. *Odd Fellows Monitor and Guide, Containing History of the Degree of Rebekah, and Its Teachings, Emblems of the Order, According to Present Classification, and Teachings of Ritual, As Understood by Obligated Odd Fellows and their Wives, With A Brief History of Our Examples, In Three Parts.* Robert Douglass, Indianapolis, 1878.

Cirlot, Juan Eduardo. *A Dictionary of Symbols.* Translated by Jack Sage. Philosophical Library, New York, 1962.

Cross, Jeremy L. *The True Masonic Chart or Hieroglyphic Monitor Containing All the Emblems Explained in the Degrees of Entered Apprentice, Fellow Craft, Master Mason, Mark Master, Past Master, Most Excellent Master, Royal Arch, Royal Master, and Select Master.* Engraved and Printed for the Author, New Haven, 1824.

Ferguson, George. *Signs & Symbols in Christian Art.* Oxford University Press, New York, 1954.

Franco, Barbara. *Masonic Symbolism in American Decorative Arts.* Scottish Rite Masonic Museum and Library, Lexington, Mass., 1976.

_____. *Fraternally Yours.* Scottish Rite Masonic Museum and Library, Lexington, Mass., 1986.

Peroni, Laura. *The Language of Flowers.* Crown, New York, 1982.

Sienkiewicz, Elly. *Spoken Without a Word: A Lexicon of Selected Symbols with 24 Patterns from Classic Baltimore Album Quilts.* Published by the author, Washington, D.C., 1983.

Spencer, F. *Chrismons, An Explanation of the Symbols on the Chrismons Tree at the Ascension Lutheran Church in Danville, Virginia.* Womack Press, Danville, Va., 1970.

PICTURES OF APPLIQUÉD ALBUM QUILTS

Allen, Gloria Seaman. *Old Line Traditions, Maryland Women and Their Quilts.* DAR Museum, Washington, D.C., 1985.

Bacon, Lenice Ingram. *American Patchwork Quilts.* Morrow, New York, 1973.

Bank, Mirra, compiler. *Anonymous Was a Woman.* St. Martin's Press, New York, 1979.

Bath, Virginia. *Needlework in America: History, Designs, and Techniques.* Viking Press, New York, 1979.

Betterton, Shiela. *Quilts and Coverlets from the American Museum in Britain.* Butler & Tanner, London, 1978, 1982.

Bishop, Robert. *The Knopf Collectors' Guides to American Antiques.* Knopf, New York, 1982.

_____. *New Discoveries in American Quilts.* Dutton, New York, 1975.

Bullard, Lacy Folmar, and Shiell, Betty Jo. *Chintz Quilts: Unfading Glory.* Serendipity Publishers, Tallahassee, Fla., 1983.

Fox, Sandi. *Small Endearments: Nineteenth-Century Quilts for Children.* Scribner, New York, 1985.

Hinson, Dolores. *American Graphic Quilt Designs.* Arco, New York, 1983.

Houck, Carter, and Nelson, Cyril. *The Quilt Engagement Calendar Treasury.* Dutton, New York, 1982.

Katzenberg, Dena. *Baltimore Album Quilts.* Baltimore Museum of Art, Baltimore, Md., 1981.

Kolter, Jane Bentley. *Forget Me Not: A Gallery of Friendship and Album Quilts.* Main Street Press, Pittstown, N.J., 1985.

Lasansky, Jeannette. *In the Heart of Pennsylvania.* Oral Traditions Project of the Union County Historical Society, Lewisburg, Pa., 1985.

_____. *In the Heart of Pennsylvania, Symposium Papers.* Oral Traditions Project of the Union County Historical Society, Lewisburg, Pa., 1986.

_____. *Pieced by Mother: Over One Hundred Years of Quiltmaking Traditions.* Oral Traditions Project of the Union

County Historical Society, Lewisburg, Pa., 1987.

Lipman, Jean, and Winchester, Alice. *The Flowering of American Folk Art, 1776–1876*. Running Press, Philadelphia, Pa., 1974.

Orlofsky, Patsy and Myron. *Quilts in America*. McGraw-Hill, New York, 1974.

Quilt Digest. Numbers 1 and 2. Kiracofe and Kile, San Francisco, 1983, 1984.

Quilt Digest. Numbers 3, 4, and 5. Quilt Digest Press, San Francisco, 1987.

Rumford, Beatrix T., and Weekley, Carolyn J. *Treasures of American Folk Art: from the Abby Aldrich Rockefeller Folk Art Center*. Little, Brown, Boston, 1989.

Safford, Carleton, and Bishop, Robert. *America's Quilts and Coverlets*. Weathervane Books/Dutton, New York, 1972.

Smyth, Frances P., and Yakush, Mary, editors. *An American Sampler: Folk Art from the Shelburne Museum*. National Gallery of Art, Washington, D.C., 1987.

Ungerleider-Mayerson, Joy. J*ewish Folk Art from Biblical Days to Modern Times*. Summit Books, New York, 1986.

Woodward, Thomas, and Greenstein, Blanche. *Crib Quilts and Other Small Wonders*. Dutton, New York, 1981.

BALTIMORE ALBUM QUILT PATTERNS AND APPLIQUÉ HOW-TO

Boyink, Betty. *Flower Gardens and Hexagons for Quilters*. Published by the author, Grand Haven, Mich., 1984.

Hinson, Dolores. *American Graphic Quilt Designs*. Arco, New York, 1983.

Kimball, Jeana. *Reflections of Baltimore*. That Patchwork Place, Bothell, Wash., 1989.

Patera, Charlotte. *Cutwork Appliqué*. New Century, Pittstown, N.J., 1983.

Sienkiewicz, Elly. *Spoken Without a Word: A Lexicon of Selected Symbols with 24 Patterns from Classic Baltimore Album Quilts*. Published by the author, Washington, D.C., 1983.

_____. *Baltimore Beauties and Beyond: Studies in Classic Album Quilt Appliqué, Volume I*. C&T Publishing, Lafayette, Calif., 1989.

Appendix I: Complex Pattern Appliqué

Baltimore Beauties and Beyond, Volume I, presented a wide range of methods for pattern transfer and appliqué. I'd like to suggest the method I find both easiest and the most foolproof for the very complex Victorian blocks, such as several of the four-page blocks shown here in "Part Two: The Patterns." This method takes more preparation before you sew, but it makes the sewing and placement relatively carefree.

When I design my own blocks, I find myself inevitably drawn to those I can begin on a cutwork base. For this method, use the directions from Lessons 1 and 2 in *Volume I*. When I am copying a pre-drawn pattern with many separate pieces, I prefer a method taught to me by Kate Fowle.

Basically, Kate uses the "freezer paper inside" method from *Volume I* (Lesson 10, Method #6). Instructions there describe how to iron the seam allowance under and have it stick to the freezer paper template inside the appliqué motif. Kate adds this step: using a lightbox, trace the complete pattern very lightly onto the block's background fabric with a fine, hard mechanical pencil. With needleturn appliqué (which tends to shrink the shape), drawing directly on the block runs the risk of showing after the appliqué is finished. Because the freezer paper template keeps the fabric held out to the exact shape of the drawn pattern, your appliqué pieces will cover the drawn lines exactly and not shrink. Try any one or all of the several freezer paper methods taught in *Volume I* (including needleturn with freezer paper on top, needleturn with freezer paper inside, or English paper method with freezer paper). With even modest care, the pencil lines won't show at all after you are done. Kate iron-bastes the uncovered shiny freezer paper template (Lesson 10, Method #6) back directly onto her appliqué shapes drawn on the background block, so that they fit exactly. Sometimes she adds an extra dab of gluestick on the shiny backing and irons that down dry, too, for a super-baste. The only drawback to iron-basting, for me, is that it needs to be done piece by piece, after the preceding piece has been sewn. If you prefer to sit still and work out of an envelope of prepared shapes, simply pin-baste as you go.

My personal preference is to use freezer paper templates but to modify the approach so that little time is spent ironing. I iron just enough to get the shape, leaving points and inward corners loose to do by simple needleturn. Even faster is to use freezer paper-underneath (Lesson 10, Method #4) but don't bother basting—just needleturn against it—or freezer paper-on-top (Lesson 2). The basic point is, *any* freezer paper method will work to keep your shapes from shrinking.

The one drawback in this approach is that it presumes your block is totally pre-planned as to fabric and color. Where one shape is repeated multiple times, such as the leaves in Pattern #15, I prepare half a dozen or so more shape units than called for. This gives me more options for perfecting the fabric and color choices as I progress on the sewing. Either Grapevine Wreath II (Pattern #15) or Folk Art Flower Wheel (Pattern #8) would be great blocks on which to introduce yourself to all the possibilities of freezer paper appliqué on a pre-marked background.

Appendix II: Course Descriptions

The following descriptions of ten possible quilting classes use *Baltimore Beauties and Beyond, Volume I* as a textbook and *Baltimore Album Quilts—Historic Notes and Antique Patterns* as the pattern source. Anyone who would like to teach these course formats or who would like to use these descriptions and materials lists has the author's and the publisher's permission to do so. Appropriate author/book credit would be appreciated. The books' copyright notices, however, prohibit photocopying or other printing of any other material herein, including patterns.

I. A HALF-DAY OR EVENING (THREE-HOUR) COURSE

"Buying for Your Baltimore Beauty." Don't know where to start? Come for a brief session on color choices, design options (relatively simple, complex, or a mixture of both) and get some pointers on which blocks would be easiest to start on. Bring your ideas, excitements, pictures, and problems! With the swatch kit provided, your shopping, whenever you choose to do it, will be much better informed and your ideas on where and how to start will be better focused as well. We'll include a lesson in capturing the special effects of the classic Baltimore look with ready-to-buy contemporary fabrics.

Materials: A swatch kit of two or three red/off-white/green color schemes will be for sale. It will also include a good blue, yellow, and pink in several shades for a multicolor quilt, plus a few special fabrics which help replicate the unique look of Baltimore. Bring pencil and paper, *Baltimore Beauties, Volume I* and *Baltimore Album Quilts—Historic Notes and Antique Patterns,* plus any pictures and ideas you have to share. Turn that dream into an heirloom Album Quilt!

II. A TWO HALF-DAY OR TWO EVENING (TWO TO THREE HOURS) COURSE

"The Heirloom Challenge—Beginning a Complex Classic Album Quilt Block." Together, we'll discuss the best fabric choice, mark the background, and make the freezer paper templates to start the dove and branch center of the exquisite cover block, "Wreath and Dove," Pattern #55 from *Baltimore Album Quilts—Historic Notes and Antique Patterns.* We will use the complex appliqué pattern transfer method from Appendix I and try multiple freezer paper template methods. The second session will focus on making the wreath and will include practice in doing the inked embellishments.

Materials: Use "Wreath and Dove II" (Pattern #55 from *Baltimore Album Quilts—Historic Notes and Antique Patterns*). You'll also need a 16" off-white 100% cotton background square (not muslin); fabrics for the appliqués on this block; a fine, hard mechanical pencil and a lightbox, or dressmaker's tracing paper and a ballpoint pen; freezer paper; fine papercutting and fabric scissors; iron and board; thread to match fabrics; #11 appliqué needles; sewing kit; and *Baltimore Beauties, Volume I* and *Baltimore Album Quilts—Historic Notes and Antique Patterns.* Note: This would go most smoothly if a well-chosen fabric kit were optionally provided.

III. AN ALL-DAY (FIVE TO SIX HOURS) COURSE

"Superfine Stems and Perfect Grapes." Begin the intriguing "Grapevine Wreath II" (Pattern #15 from quilt #1, shown in the Color Section of *Baltimore Album Quilts—Historic Notes and Antique Patterns*). Learn the superfine stem method, how to make perfect grapes, and how to use a marked background fabric and freezer paper appliqué motif templates. This relatively simple block is perfect for learning an approach which will sail you through the most complex blocks. Moreover, its leaf and grape color scheme invites you to try your hand at dramatic fabric choice.

Materials: Use "Grapevine Wreath II" (Pattern #15 from *Baltimore Album Quilts—Historic Notes and Antique Patterns*). You will need a handful of greens and purples (or blues, or reds—your choice of grapes); thread to match; a 16" background block with the pattern very carefully and lightly traced onto it with a hard sharp pencil; freezer paper; file cards for grape templates; an architectural small circle template (or a coin of appropriate size); ¾" masking tape; #11 appliqué needles; sewing kit; and *Baltimore Beauties, Volume I* and *Baltimore Album Quilts—Historic Notes and Antique Patterns.*

IV. A THREE HALF-DAY OR THREE EVENING COURSE (THREE THREE-HOUR CLASSES)

"Introduction to Baltimore Album Quilts: One, Two, Four...And Then You're Ready For More!" From beginner to advanced, you'll love this introduction to the methods and patterns presented in *Baltimore Beauties and Beyond*. Using patterns from *Baltimore Album Quilts—Historic Notes and Antique Patterns,* we'll start simply, on Fleur-de-Lis II (Pattern #2, given on one page). We'll progress to "Folk Art Vase of Flowers" (Pattern #34, on two pages), and then to "Albertine's Rose Climber" (Pattern #39, on four pages), taking you through a multitude of appliqué methods. By completion of these blocks you will have added fine cutwork appliqué stems, freezer paper inside method, perfect circles, layered flowers, inlaid tulips, embroidered roses, and inked inscriptions to your basic cutwork appliqué technique.

Materials for the first class: Bring one 16" square each of off-white background fabric, and a medium-to-large predominantly red print; thread to match; dressmaker's tracing (carbon) paper and ballpoint pen; freezer paper (optional if you choose to use Lesson 2 rather than Lesson 1 for the Fleur-de-Lis II block); papercutting and fabric scissors; iron and board; #11 appliqué needles; sewing kit; and *Baltimore Beauties, Volume I* and *Baltimore Album Quilts—Historic Notes and Antique Patterns*. Material lists for the second and third session will be discussed in class.

V. A THREE HALF-DAY OR THREE EVENING COURSE (THREE THREE-HOUR CLASSES)

"Victoria Green, Turkey Red, and the Heyday of Appliqué." These colors unite the classic Baltimore Albums and will enhance your quilt with only a moderate input of time. Make three red and green blocks: "Victorian Favorite" (Pattern #11), "Hearts and Tulips" (Pattern #9), and "Red Vases and Red Flowers" (Pattern #10). These will acquaint you thoroughly with the joys of two-color cutwork with and without freezer paper-on-top, perfect points and smooth curves, cutwork appliqué stems, and reverse and onlaid appliqué. Intermediate—Advanced.

Materials for the first class: Bring one 16" square each of an off-white background fabric, and a Victoria green; scraps of red; dressmaker's tracing (carbon) paper and ballpoint pen; freezer paper; papercutting and fabric scissors; iron and board; thread to match; #11 appliqué needles; sewing kit; and *Baltimore Beauties, Volume I* and *Baltimore Album Quilts—Historic Notes and Antique Patterns*.

VI. A FOUR ALL-DAY OR EIGHT EVENING COURSE (EIGHT THREE-HOUR CLASSES)

"Big on Baltimore Baskets." The basket motif was often repeated in the classic Album Quilts and is appealing in the nine-block center with four baskets balanced against each other. We'll take on the challenge of baskets, birds, bows, and layered flowers together as we make four lovely Victorian basket blocks, each well begun in class. If you have a yen for originality, you can weave your baskets, braid their rims, intertwine ribbon, or incorporate your own creative variation on these classic patterns. This is a class for the serious appliquér who loves handwork!

Materials: Baltimore Album Quilts—Historic Notes and Antique Patterns ("Victorian Basket of Flowers IV," Pattern #41, and "Victorian Basket V with Fruits and Flowers," Pattern #42, or, optionally, Pattern #40), *Baltimore Beauties and Beyond, Volume I* ("Red Woven Basket of Flowers," Pattern #26), and *Spoken Without a Word* (for the pattern "Basket with Blooms, Bird, and Bible"); 18" square of background fabric with Pattern #41 lightly traced on it in hard pencil; appliqué fabric and threads to match; floral and leaf shapes traced off onto freezer paper; gluestick; #11 appliqué needles; scissors for fabric and paper; file cards; sewing kit; and *Baltimore Beauties, Volume I, Baltimore Album Quilts—Historic Notes and Antique Patterns*, and *Spoken Without a Word*. If you can find a fine woven cord or soutache braid in the color you want your basket, you may be able to use it. For each basket we will spend the first class marking background fabric and preparing appliqués. The second class for each basket will deal with any technical issues on the in-progress block.

VII. A FOUR HALF-DAY OR FOUR EVENING COURSE (FOUR THREE-HOUR CLASSES)

" 'The Album': An Exquisite Classic Baltimore Block For the Very Busy!" In four well-spaced evenings, this class takes you through the making of a very beautiful, very complex block. Each week, all the preparation will be done in class, so that you have a kit ready to sew in your all-too-few spare moments. Savor this advanced appliqué learned at a slower pace and finish aglow with pride!

Materials for the first class: Baltimore Album Quilts—Historic Notes and Antique Patterns (Pattern #46, "The Album"); you'll also need freezer paper to trace the pattern in class and either a lightbox or dressmaker's tracing (carbon) paper to transfer it to your block; a 16" square of background fabric; hard mechanical pencil; appliqué fabric and threads to match; iron. We'll cut out the freezer paper shapes and prepare our appliqué motifs for sewing by one or more of the freezer paper template appliqué methods. Other materials needed throughout the class: gluestick; #11 appliqué needles; fine scissors for fabric and paper; file cards; sewing kit; and *Baltimore Album Quilts—Historic Notes and Antique*

Patterns. (Note: If a kit in wonderful fabrics could be available, this would be a great help to a busy person. In addition, a simple "lightbox" can easily be made: you'll need a 16" square of Plexiglass (to prop between lap and table) and a small lamp (to hold between the knees). Or use a shallow square cardboard box, Plexiglass cut to cover, and an inexpensive fluorescent light on a cord, such as a "Stick O' Light."™)

VIII. A ONE-YEAR COURSE (TEN THREE-HOUR CLASSES)

"Designing and Making the Classic Nine-Block Baltimore Album Quilt Center." The fanciest blocks were traditionally the center nine blocks of a twenty-five-block set. There, their magnificence was well displayed on the middle of the bed. Meet for one class on designing your center nine, then create one block a month, to completion. Quilts #2 and #6 from *Volume I* are models of fancy nine-block centers. Or perhaps you'd like to simply make one fabulous quilt of nine blocks.

Materials for the first class: You'll need graph paper; pencil; gluestick; paper scissors; swatches of your main color scheme; freezer paper and pattern to trace templates. Bring photocopies of Baltimore Album Quilts that focus on the nine center blocks. Bring duplicate photocopies (so you can play with layouts) of blocks which make good corners to a nine-block center: blocks with strong diagonals, open wreaths, crossed sprays, etc. Include blocks you think would make a good center block (often used for the quilt's dedication). Bring *Baltimore Beauties, Volume I* and *Baltimore Album Quilts—Historic Notes and Antique Patterns* (also *Spoken Without a Word* for the baskets and diagonal cornucopia), and freezer paper so you can begin tracing off the first pattern if time allows.

IX. A ONE-YEAR COURSE (TEN THREE-HOUR CLASSES)

"A Block-a-Month: Ten Favorite Victorian Album Quilt Motifs." They loved them then, we love them now: the Rose of Sharon, sprays of flowers, baskets, vases, ribbon-tied bouquets, broken wreaths, circular wreaths, cornucopias, lyres, and birds. Begin with a red, green, and yellow block, "Asymmetrical Spray of Red Blossoms I" (Pattern #37 from *Baltimore Album Quilts—Historic Notes and Antique Patterns*) and progress to more complex appliqués.

Materials for the first class: You'll need a 16" square each of off-white, red, and green fabric; scraps of yellow; green thread; freezer paper; file cards; paper and fabric scissors; dressmaker's tracing (carbon) paper; iron; sewing kit; *Baltimore Beauties, Volume I* and *Baltimore Album Quilts—Historic Notes and Antique Patterns*. Note to class teachers: The green can be most easily done by cutwork (Lesson 2 in *Volume I*), the red by freezer paper on top (or freezer paper inside, Lesson 10), the circles with a file card template inside (Lesson 9).

X. A ONE-YEAR COURSE (TEN THREE-HOUR CLASSES)

"Fascinating Ladies: A Baltimore Album Quilt Support Group." The group—its challenge, support, insights, inspirations—is supposed by many scholars to have been a major ingredient in the unparalleled heights reached by mid-nineteenth-century Baltimore Album quiltmakers. Recreate the ambience and get your quilt well underway with help and encouragement from the area's finest talents!

Materials for the first class: Whatever stage you're at—just beginning or mid-way through—bring pencil, paper, a set of your Album Quilt fabric swatches, pictures, and a block to begin or work on. Bring your ideas, questions, problems to share, and of course, *Baltimore Beauties, Volume I* and *Baltimore Album Quilts—Historic Notes and Antique Patterns*. Ladies of the Club, come for fun and a more fabulous quilt!

Appendix III: *Sources*

If, after checking with your local quilt shop, you are still looking for a special service or supply, this brief listing may help.

BOOKS

Baltimore Beauties and Beyond, Studies in Classic Album Quilt Appliqué, Volume I, by Elly Sienkiewicz. $23.95 softcover, $39.95 hardcover; plus $2 shipping. C&T Publishing, P.O. Box 1456, Lafayette, CA 94549, 1-800-284-1114.

Baltimore Album Quilts—Historic Notes and Antique Patterns: A Pattern Companion to Baltimore Beauties, Volume I, by Elly Sienkiewicz. $23.95 softcover, plus $2 shipping. C&T Publishing, P.O. Box 1456, Lafayette, CA 94549, 1-800-284-1114.

Down Home Needleart to the Museum Walls, by Hazel B. Reed Ferrell. A compendium of original quilting designs plus a few patchwork patterns, self-published. Hazel designed and quilted *Volume I's* quilt #7. Closeups of her quilting and designs can be seen on the front and back covers of that volume. $14.95, plus $1 postage/handling. Hazel B. Reed Ferrell, Route 1, Box 144, Middlebourne, WV 26149.

Friendship's Offering: Techniques and Inspiration for Writing on Quilts, by Susan McKelvey. $15.95, plus $2.00 shipping. C & T Publishing, P.O. Box 1456, Lafayette, CA 94549, 1-800-284-1114.

Spoken Without a Word: A Lexicon of Selected Symbols with 24 Patterns from Classic Baltimore Album Quilts, by Elly Sienkiewicz. $18.95, plus $3 shipping. Elly Sienkiewicz, 5540 30th Street NW, Washington, DC 20015.

SUPPLIES

The Cotton Patch. A good source for Hemmings needles, including #11 Sharps and #10 English Milliners Straw Needles (these were suggested by Helen Oelkrug, Carrollton, Texas, and Roslyn Kempston, Richardson, Texas). An intriguing collection of sophisticated prints and background fabrics are included in The Cotton Patch's 300 swatches for $3. An extensive mail-order catalog, minus the swatches, is free. The Cotton Patch, 1025 Brown Avenue, Lafayette, CA 94549.

New York Beauty Fabric and Design. Hand-dyed fabric. For information and price list, send large self-addressed, stamped envelope. New York Beauty Fabric and Design, 610 Hamilton Parkway, DeWitt, NY 13214.

Pepper Cory's Background Quilting Templates for Classic Appliqué. Four separate 16" square all-over quilting designs to fill the white space behind appliqué blocks. Items #PC-22 through PC-25. Quilting Creations, Box 508, Zoar, OH 44697, 216-874-4741.

Tie-dyed Fabrics by Marty Lawrence. For information and price list, send large self-addressed, stamped envelope. Marty Lawrence, P. O. Box 4602, Flint, MI 48504.

True Colors. Carol Esch's hand-dyed fabric, sets of graduated saturations of color, marbleized fabric. Send large self-addressed, stamped envelope for free catalog. Carol Esch, RD 3, Box 78, Pittstown, NJ 08398.

About the Author

Elly Sienkiewicz's fascination with the Baltimore Album Quilts combines old loves—history, religion, and art—and is now of many years' duration. In 1983, Elly self-published *Spoken Without a Word: A Lexicon of Selected Symbols with 24 Patterns from Classic Baltimore Album Quilts*. Winners of a contest based on that book became latter-day "Ladies of Baltimore," an ongoing and growing group. Through their help, Elly has produced several appliqué Album Quilts shown in these volumes. She draws upon over two dozen years of teaching experience in writing *Baltimore Beauties and Beyond, Volume I*, and *Baltimore Album Quilts—Historic Notes and Antique Patterns*.

Elly received a Bachelor of Arts degree in History from Wellesley College, and a Masters of Science in Education from the University of Pennsylvania. After teaching secondary school history and English for seven years, she went on maternity leave with her first born, and never returned to school teaching. Staying at home with her young children, Elly pursued a number of enterprises, including starting (with partner Betty Martin) the mail-order quilt supply business Cabin Fever Calicoes. She sold the business after seven years (1978–85), allowing her time to pursue her interest in teaching and writing about Baltimore Album Quilts. Elly's first book in this series, is *Baltimore Beauties and Beyond, Studies in Classic Album Quilt Appliqué, Volume I*.

She lives in Washington, D.C., with her husband Stan, and children, Donald Hamilton, Alex Corbly, and Eileen Katherine (Katya) Hamilton Sienkiewicz.

ABOUT THE BACK COVER

Back Cover: *Baltimore's Monument to George Washington*. Many public buildings and monuments were depicted in the classic Baltimore Quilts and Baltimore's Monument to George Washington was a particular favorite. This version is a detail from quilt #2. See the discussion of that quilt in "Part One: The Quiltmakers." A black-and-white detail photo of the War of 1812 Monument from this same quilt appears on page 20.

Detail: Baltimore Album Quilt. Accession #76.609.6. Gift of Mr. and Mrs. Foster McCarl, Jr. 92" x 91½". (Photo: Abby Aldrich Rockefeller Folk Art Center, Williamsburg, Virginia)

Other fine quilting books from C&T Publishing:

A Celebration of Hearts
Jean Wells and Marina Anderson

An Amish Adventure
Roberta Horton

Baltimore Beauties and Beyond
Elly Sienkiewicz

Boston Commons Quilt
Blanche Young and Helen Young Frost

Calico and Beyond
Roberta Horton

Contemporary Sampler
Katie Pasquini

Crazy Quilt Handbook
Judith Montano

Crosspatch
Pepper Cory

Diamond Patchwork
Jeffrey Gutcheon

Fans
Jean Wells

Fine Feathers
Marianne Fons

Flying Geese Quilt
Blanche Young and Helen Young Frost

Friendship's Offering
Susan McKelvey

Heirloom Machine Quilting
Harriet Hargrave

Irish Chain Quilt
Blanche Young and Helen Young Frost

Landscapes and Illusions
Joen Wolfrom

Let's Make Waves
Marianne Fons and Liz Porter

Light and Shadows
Susan McKelvey

Mandala
Katie Pasquini

Mariner's Compass
Judy Mathieson

New Lone Star Handbook
Blanche Young and Helen Young Frost

Perfect Pineapples
Jane Hall and Dixie Haywood

Picture This
Jean Wells and Marina Anderson

Plaids and Stripes
Roberta Horton

Quilting Designs From the Amish
Pepper Cory

Quilting Designs From Antique Quilts
Pepper Cory

Radiant Nine Patch
Blanche Young

Stained Glass Quilting Technique
Roberta Horton

Trip Around the World Quilts
Blanche Young and Helen Young Frost

Visions: Quilts of a New Decade
Quilt San Diego

Working in Miniature
Becky Schaefer

Wearable Art For Real People
Mary Mashuta

3 Dimensional Design
Katie Pasquini

For more information write for a free catalog from:
C & T Publishing
P.O. Box 1456
Lafayette, CA 94553